Cover photo by Peter Klavora:
Joakim Dreifke, world and Olympic champion,
doubles and quad; 1976 Olympic bronze medalist, singles.

THE COMPLETE SCULLER

THE COMPLETE SCULLER

RICHARD BURNELL

Sport Books Publisher Toronto

Canadian Cataloguing in Publication Data

Burnell, Richard
The complete sculler

2nd ed.
ISBN 0-920905-14-5

1. Rowing. I. Title.

GV791.B87 1989   797.1'23   C89-093366-9

Distribution in Canada and world wide by
Sport Books Publisher
278 Robert Street
Toronto, Canada M5S 2K8

Printed in the United States

CONTENTS

INTRODUCTION

To be asked for a reprint of a sculling book which was first published fifteen years ago, and which was even then a distillation of several earlier books on the same subject, is gratifying, but in some respects daunting. One must ask oneself – because others will certainly ask the same question – 'Is this still valid, and does it still meet a genuine need?'

To answer the second question first, all of my previous sculling books have had the same aim, which is to make good the deficiency of sculling coaching. Do not misunderstand this. I am not suggesting that those professionals, and the few amateurs, who regularly coach scullers, do not make a good job of it. There is photographic evidence in these pages to prove that they certainly do. But the number of men and women, from junior up to veteran status sculling today is vastly greater than it was a few decades ago, and shows no sign of declining. And all too often they get little if any coaching, even when they are being required to scull as part of the selection process for rowing in a crew. There is a lot of coaching for rowing and not a few textbooks on the subject, but the sculler is left to his own devices.

So I believe the need for a sculling book is indisputable. But is the advice which was offered in 1975 still valid today, or has it been outdated by more advanced equipment and techniques?

In my youth there used to be several different ways of rowing – at risk of over simplification, Orthodoxy, Fairbairnism, Conibear and so on. But one thing which I soon noticed was that irrespective of their labels, the better crews got the more similar they looked. The change I notice in rowing between yesterday and today is that nobody argues about style any more.

There have never been the same arguments about sculling. It is a more efficient, and in some respects more demanding method of propelling a boat than rowing. Fads and heresies have not flourished because, quite simply, only the right methods of sculling have ever achieved any success. So I believe the advice offered in 1975 would have passed muster fifty years before, and I shall be surprised if it is not still sound in the year 2000. Perhaps by then sculling coaching will be taken seriously, and the need for a simple D.I.Y. textbook will have receded. But I doubt it.

Since I wrote in 1975 there has certainly been one major change in the sport, and that has been the enormous increase in the number of people building sculling boats, and marketing the associated equipment. This must be good because it means competition and innovation. It does not outdate the Theory of Rigging as propounded in Chapter I of this book; but it does outdate some of my comments on the methods of adjustment, particularly with reference to the diagramatic drawing of the Swivel Rowlock on page 30, nor would it be possible to illustrate all the alternatives available today.

There is another point which arises from the wide choice of equipment now available. It becomes ever easier to make instant adjustments. The leverage on the sculls, the span, the height of the work, the pitch of the swivels, the sculler's position in the boat, can all be altered in a few minutes. With so many variables from which to choose the sculler is inevitably tempted to adjust the rig whenever things are not going well. He or she may just be right of course, particularly since the boat is frequently transported on the roof of a car, and rigged and unrigged several times in a week. But it is well to remember that by far the most variable of all the factors involved is the person doing the sculling. A sculler may be unable to catch the beginning of the stroke efficiently because he is heavy handed or unbalanced. Increasing the severity of the rig may indeed assist the sculler to get hold of the water; but it will not cure the fault nor bring much joy when the headwind starts to blow.

There is no more important advice in this book than this, elementary though it may appear. If something seems to be wrong, first try another pair of sculls in your boat, or try your own sculls in another boat, or get another sculler to try your sculls in your boat. If it turns out that there is a fault in the rigging, and not in your technique, that is the moment to start making rigging adjustments – one at a time. If on the other hand you are sufficiently confident and experienced to do without such trials, then perhaps you have already taken the first steps on the way to becoming a 'Complete Sculler.' But do not take it for granted!

I

RIGGING

'To catch well, and to finish well'

A HUNDRED AND THIRTY YEARS AGO, most sculling boats were still working boats, used for transporting goods and passengers, and roomy and strong accordingly. The seat was a plank of wood, the stretcher another plank, and the rowlock a pin, or a pair of pins, fixed to the gunwhale. The only moveable part was the stretcher, which could be set to suit the length of the sculler's legs.

If a waterman wished to race, which he sometimes did with great profit, he looked for a lighter, and, if possible, narrower boat. But as the rowlocks were part of the gunwhales, the overall width of the boat could not be reduced without also reducing the 'span', that is, the distance between the rowlocks. And reducing the span meant using shorter sculls, and losing leverage.

The only solution to this problem was to build a boat as narrow as possible on the waterline, with widely flared gunwhales. This produced a top-heavy and unstable craft.

Then, in 1844, the Newcastle-on-Tyne boatbuilder, Henry Clasper, made the first 'outrigger', using iron rods to support the rowlocks. This was the key to the science of rigging. The waterman could now use longer sculls, and discovered that he could scull a longer stroke by moving backwards and forwards on his seat. The single plank was replaced by a platform of polished wood. This was sometimes covered with grease, or soft soap, and trousers were reinforced with leather padding. It worked, in a messy and uncomfortable way, at least until the lubrication dried up.

In 1857, J. C. Babcock, of the Nassau Boat Club, New York, invented the sliding seat. It was another twelve years before a satisfactory model was produced. But the sliding seat was the natural complement to the outrigger, and, between them, the two inventions revolutionised sculling.

Writing in *The New York Spirit of the Times*, on 4th January 1873, Babcock explained his reasoning: '. . . to catch well and to finish well . . . the rowlock should be moved . . . backwards and forwards each stroke . . . as this was impractical, the idea of moving the seat occurred to me.'

Hence the quotation at the head of this chapter. 'To catch well and to finish well' is, indeed, the sculler's objective. Rigging is the method by which he can attain it.

'*Rigging consists of adjusting the moveable parts of the boat so that the sculler is comfortable, and favourably placed to scull hard.*' This sentence has appeared in all my previous sculling books, and I can still offer no better brief description.

It is not possible to lay down, definitively, all the correct measurements for an individual sculler. For rigging is an individual matter, depending on the sculler's shape, strength, and size. Also it is closely linked to technique, and to the particular job in hand. Not every man who is 6 ft. tall has the same length arms. A 13-stone man is not necessarily stronger than a $12\frac{1}{2}$-stone man. A rig which is suitable for the British Amateur Sculling Championship, raced over $4\frac{1}{4}$ miles, on the tideway, may be quite unsuitable for the Diamond Sculls at Henley.

This chapter sets out to establish what the rigging options are, and how they can be exercised. First, then, let us look at the variable factors in rigging.

1. **The Stretcher** is variable as to fore and aft position in the boat, height above the floor, vertical angle with the floor, and the angle between the feet.

2. **The Slide Bed** (i.e. the track) is variable as to length, fore and aft position, and angle of incline to the horizontal.

3. **The Seat** is variable as to fore and aft position relative to the rowlocks, and as to height above the heels, or floor of the boat.

4. **The Frontstop and Backstop** are variable as limiting factors to the movement of the seat.

5. **The Rowlocks** are variable as to fore and aft position, vertical position, pitch (angle relative to the vertical from the water), and distance from the centre line of the boat.

6. **The Sculls** are variable as to overall length, the position of the buttons (which determines the inboard and outboard length), the shape and size of the blades, and the degree of rigidity of the looms.

We must consider these factors in greater detail. But first we can look at the Rigging Table, and at Figs. I–III.

As regards the figures in the Rigging Table, I cannot over-emphasise the fact that they are intended as, and can only be, guidelines. I do not claim that any particular measurement, taken from the Table, will necessarily be right for any individual sculler. But I do claim that any substantial departure from these measurements will be a departure from well tried and proven experience.

I have already said that rigging is closely linked to technique. It is not simply a matter of making a sculler comfortable, but also of making him efficient. It follows that rigging is not static, but constantly developing. One recommends such-and-such a measurement, to enable a sculler to do so-and-so. The requirement changes all the time, be it only for a minor adjustment, to suit changing conditions of wind and water.

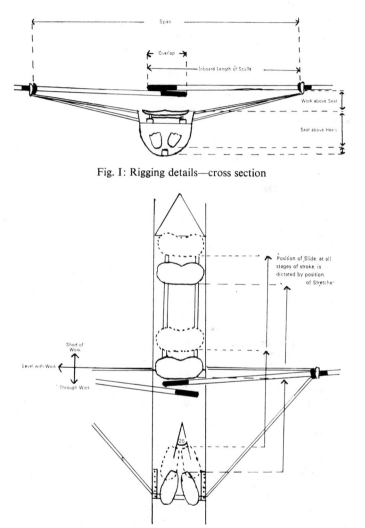

Fig. I: Rigging details—cross section

Fig. II: Rigging details—plan

RIGGING TABLE

Height of Sculler	5′ 6″ (167 cm.)	5′ 9″ (175 cm.)	6′ 0″ (183 cm.)	6′ 3″ (190 cm.)
Heels above bottom of boat	About 1½ in. (4 cm.) with fixed stretcher, and somewhat more when hinged track shoes are used.			
Seat above heels	6¾–7½ in. (17–19 cm.) with fixed stretcher 5½–6¾ in. (14–17 cm.) with hinged track shoes			
Work above seat	3½–6½ in. (9–17 cm.)			
Frontstop	1½ in. (4 cm.) through to 1½ in. (4 cm.) short of work.			
Sliding	16–18 in. (41–46 cm.)		18–20 in. (46–51 cm.)	
Span	4′ 9″ (145 cm.)	4′ 10″ (147 cm.)	4′ 11″ (150 cm.)	5′ 0″ (152 cm.)
Sculls Overall	9′ 5″ (287 cm.)	9′ 6½″ (291 cm.)	9′ 8″ (294 cm.)	9′ 10″ (300 cm.)
Sculls Inboard	2′ 8½″ (83 cm.)	2′ 9¼″ (85 cm.)	2′ 9¾″ (86 cm.)	2′ 10½″ (87 cm.)
Overlap of Handles	8–9 in. (20–23 cm.)			
Blades	A modern scull blade will be 19–20 in. (48–51 cm.) long, 5½–6¼ in. (14–17 cm.) wide at the tip, with a maximum width of 6½–7¾ in. (17–21 cm.) at a distance of 5–8 in. (13–20 cm.) from the tip. The blade area should be between 105–120 sq. in. (677–774 sq. cm.)			

see footnote page 17.

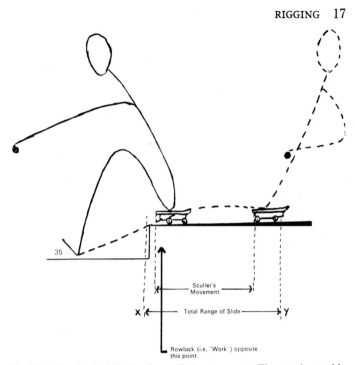

Fig. III: The physical limits of a sculler's movement. The seat is capable of moving forward to point 'x', and backward to point 'y'. By moving his stretcher aft the sculler could also reach point 'x'. But he could not increase the distance he slides, which is limited by the length of his legs.

Rowing Magazine (Vol. 18, No. 213, January–February 1973) published a list of sculling rigs as used at the Munich Olympics. These rigs were used by some of the strongest and most experienced scullers in the world, at that time, which accounts for some of the measurements being more severe than any suggested in the Table above.

However all such published rigs need to be treated with caution, unless they are accompanied by diagrams, or a clear indication of how the measurements were taken, as there is, unfortunately, no standard practice in measuring and describing rigging.   To quote two examples, some take the "length of slide" to be the "length of track", whilst others take it to be the "distance which the seat moves", or even the "distance which the seat *can* move", "Span", too, may be measured between the bearing surfaces of the tholes, or between the centres of the pins on which the tholes rotate (see page 28).

When experimenting 'by trial and error', do not alter more than one factor at a time. If a sculler moves his stretcher, shifts the buttons on his sculls, and raises the height of his rowlocks, all at the same time, he may perhaps achieve an improvement—but he will certainly not know why, which is a prerequisite for further progress.

Also it is useful to keep a written note of rigging measurements, and alterations, and to check regularly, particularly when a boat is transported by road, or used by another sculler. It is a sad fact that, if you ask a sculler, or a coach, how his boat is rigged, he will, as often as not, be quite unable to say. If he does not even know what the measurements are supposed to be, what are the chances that they will be right?

Let us then consider the rigging variables, and how to use them, in more detail.

The Stretcher.

Height above bottom of boat. The current fashion is to set the stretcher well above the bottom of the boat, on the theory that having the feet nearer to the level of the slide enables the legs to develop a more direct thrust. I doubt that this theory is sound, for the task of the legs is not to propel the seat along the track, but to drive the body backwards *and upwards*, on its arc towards the finish of the stroke. This is less, rather than more, likely to be achieved from a high set stretcher. Moreover a high stretcher contributes to instability, raising the centre of gravity, and making it more difficult to slide up towards the frontstop without constriction. The heels should be set approximately $1\frac{1}{2}$ in. (4 cm.) above the bottom of the boat.

Angle between the feet. Most people, when doing a knees-bend exercise, or picking up an object from the floor, will naturally stand with their feet splayed at an angle between 20 and 30 degrees. This gives a firm base, and encourages the knees to open naturally. The modern trend is to have less splay than this on the stretcher, with the feet sometimes almost parallel, which in my view often leads to unsteadiness.

The Rake. The rake of the stretcher is the angle which it makes with the keel. This is a valid statement for the conventional type of 'clog', which has rigid soles attached to both top and bottom stretcher bearers. But it is not really valid as applied to the new pattern of pliable track shoes, which are attached only to the top bearer, and, in effect, are therefore 'hinged'. There is no need to vary the recommendation of 30–40 degrees rake, but it is now possible for the sculler's feet to move within this range during the stroke. There are obvious advantages in the new shoes, providing they are not used simply to overcome stiff ankles.

Fore and aft adjustment. This is the basic adjustment of 'altering the stretcher'. One will sometimes hear a coach tell a man to 'bring the stretcher a hole nearer'. If you think about this for a moment you will see that this is precisely what the man cannot do, unless of course he is already jammed against his backstop—when it would be the last thing he would want to do. You cannot bring the stretcher nearer to *yourself*, because your feet are on it, and if you move it you simply move yourself with it. This is why the moving of the stretcher is one of the key variables in rigging.

The setting of the stretcher determines the position of the sculler, relative to his rowlocks, at all stages of the stroke.

Fig. IV illustrates this. Although diagramatic, the drawing is approximately to scale, the three scullers 'A', 'B', and 'C', all having the same reach. Sculler 'B' is sliding level with his work, 'A' is sliding about 3 in. (8 cm.) through (aft of) his work, and 'C' is sliding about 3 in. short of his work. At this moment we are not concerned with who is right. But we can see that, the farther the sculler slides towards the

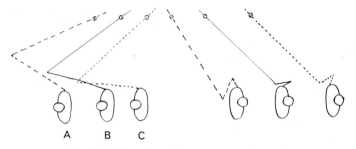

Fig. IV: Effect of moving stretcher fore and aft

stern, the more acute will be the angle at which his blades take the beginning of the stroke. And we can also see that, because 'A' is 3 in. farther forward, and 'C' is 3 in. less far forward, than 'B', at the beginning of the stroke, the same must be true at the finish, and that this affects the position of the arms, and of the sculls handles.

The Slide Bed.

The Slide Bed, that is to say the track on which the sliding seat moves, is not adjustable in the normal sense of the word. But it can be described as one of the rigging variables, in that its length, position in the boat, and angle of incline, can differ. And, as we have just seen, the sculler can exercise his choice of which part of the track he is going to use.

Length of Slide. There is sometimes confusion about the 'length' of the slide, because people persist in quoting the total length of the track as the slide length. This is ridiculous, as the farthest distance the seat can possibly 'slide' is from the point where its front wheels touch the front end of the track, to the point where its back wheels touch the back end of the track.

This distance, which I call the 'movement', is likely to be between 28 in. (71 cm.), extending backwards* from a point about 4 in. (10 cm.) aft of the work, in recently built boats, and about 24 in. (61 cm.), from a point about 2 in. (5 cm.) aft of the work, in older boats.

There will be stops, usually brass screws, at both extremities of the track, for the purpose of preventing the seat from falling off the track when the boat is being carried. The sculler should not come into contact with these screws, and, if he does so regularly, is likely to damage the wheels of his slide. If he requires a working frontstop, or backstop (which we will consider later), these will be wooden blocks, fixed to the decking.

Angle of Incline. The slide bed is usually inclined so that the forward end (nearest the bows) is $\frac{1}{2}$–$\frac{3}{4}$ in. (2 cm.) higher than the aft end. This eases the pressure of the calves of the legs on the forward edge of the decking, at the finish of the stroke, and aids the sculler in sliding forward against the run of the boat.

The Seat.

Fore and Aft Position. The movement of the seat is variable, in that the sculler can choose which part of the track he is going to use.

Height above Heels. The height of the seat above the heels is also variable, by raising or lowering either the seat

* In a book about sculling it seems to be impossible to avoid confusion over such words as 'backwards' and 'forwards', 'in front of', 'behind', etc. This is because the sculler is always said to be sliding 'forward' as he approaches the 'frontstop', although this is in the stern ('aft') of the boat, whilst his 'backstop' is 'forward' in nautical geography. I know that this is understood in British sculling, but usage is not always identical in other countries. So, just for the record:

   (i) The 'frontstop' is in the stern.
   (ii) The 'backstop' is in the bows.
   (iii) The word 'work' denotes the position of the rowlock.
   (iv) 'Through the work' means aft of the rowlock.
   (v) 'Behind the work' means between the rowlock and the bows

or the stretcher. This adjustment is usually only needed for an individual who has a very long, or very short body, or legs, or exceptionally massive calves or thighs.

Frontstop and Backstop.

A frontstop and backstop can be fitted if desired, and are necessary if the sculler is sliding right to either end of the track, to protect the wheels of the slide. If the sculler is not reaching either end of the track, then the use of working stops is a matter of preference.

The sculler should not normally come into contact with his frontstop. But if he is inclined to lose control, and to slide too far forward, a frontstop can be a useful check. If he continues to hit it, the probable remedy is to shorten the stretcher.

At the finish of the stroke it is physically impossible to slide farther back than the length of the legs allow, so nobody can slide too far back by mistake. Many coaches therefore regard a backstop as unnecessary. Others reckon that the sculler is more likely to achieve a strong finishing position, and a controlled recovery, if his seat is secured by a backstop.

My advice is that less experienced scullers should use a backstop, set so that they do not hit it, but can just feel it at the finish of the stroke. More experienced scullers can make the decision for themselves. But I can see no possible disadvantage in using a backstop, and invariably did so myself.

The Choice of Movement. The total range of slide movement is between 24 in. (61 cm.) and 28 in. (71 cm.). But I have never seen a man who could slide anything like that far. Fig. III illustrates why this is so. A six foot man (183 cm.) may measure about 40 in. (102 cm.) from pelvis to heel, or about 32 in. (81 cm.) on what the tailor refers to as 'inside leg measurement', which is much the same as the distance from his heel to the point where his buttocks touch the front edge of his seat. If the track extended all the way, and he could slide up until his buttocks touched his heels, that is the maximum distance he could move (it would, of course, entail having his heels level with the track).

As we are considering sculling, and not Yoga, it is unnecessary to point out why this is impossible. As to how far a sculler actually can slide forward, and still be able to 'spring' back from the stretcher, that is a subject on which one might argue for many hours—and the conclusion would still depend on the build and suppleness of the individual. For practical purposes I would say that a tall man can slide about 20 in. (51 cm.), and a short man about 16 in. (41 cm.).

Clearly then, if scullers can slide between 16–20 in. (41–51 cm.), and if the range of the slide is between 24–28 in. (61–71 cm.), there is a choice, and *that choice is exercised by setting the stretcher.*

Let us remember Babcock's text: *To catch well and to finish well.* So we have the objectives, and we have the options. How are they to be exercised?

It is the finishing position which is the more important. We can now look back at Figure IV, which shows the effects of finishing at different distances from the rowlocks. If the sculler is too close to his work he will be cramped, his scull handles will come into his stomach, his hands will be caught up, and he will not achieve a powerful finish and a clean recovery.

If he is too far away from his work, his scull handles will not reach his body at all. His finish will be short, and any attempt to lengthen it will either pull the scull buttons away from the rowlocks, or cause the sculler's arms to pull outwards, away from his body—a hopelessly weak position.

The correct finishing position will bring the scull handles into the body just below the ribs, and above the hip-bones.

Figure IV also shows that the farther the sculler reaches forward, at the beginning of the stroke, the more acute will be the angle between his sculls and the side of the boat. The thrust of the blades against the water is at 90 degrees to the axis of the sculls. So the only point, during the stroke, when the whole of the thrust is propelling the boat forward, is when the sculls are at 90 degrees to the centre line of the boat. Before that point, part of the thrust is wasted in pushing outwards, 'pinching the boat' we call it. And beyond that point the blades begin to thrust inwards, towards the stern of the boat.

In order to develop the maximum thrust in the middle of the stroke, when it is most effective, the sculler must take the catch well behind the rigger. But if he goes too far he will pinch the boat. His forward position will be affected by his suppleness, and the length of his arms. His finishing position will be affected by the length of his legs. There has to be some compromise at the catch, between getting an effective grip of the water, and avoiding pinching. At the finish there is less scope for compromise, because, to achieve his strong position, the sculler must be within an inch or two of the 'right' position.

In practice, therefore, the stretcher must be set so that the finishing position is right. If the catch is not then near enough satisfactory, the solution must be sought elsewhere, as we shall see in a moment, when we consider the outriggers. If, after setting the stretcher to obtain a comfortable finishing position, you find that you are sliding more than 2 in. (5 cm.) through the work, or more than 2 in. short of the work, then an alteration to the sculls, or the outriggers, is probably needed.

Finally, as this book is partly directed to rowing coaches, and to scullers who are 'sculling for rowing', a word of warning is indicated, concerning one basic difference between rowing and sculling rigging.

Figure V is drawn approximately to scale, illustrating an oarsman and a sculler, of equal height and reach, and both sliding forward level with their work. The oarsman has a leverage (distance from thole pin to the centre-line of the boat) of 31 in. (79 cm.), and an oar 3 ft. 7 in. (109 cm.) inboard. The sculler has a 5 ft. (152 cm.) span, and sculls 2 ft. 10 in. (87 cm.) inboard—both quite conventional.

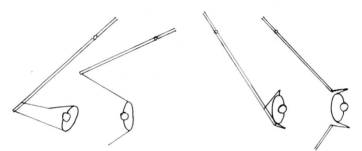

Fig. V: The difference between beginning and finishing positions of oarsmen and sculler

It will be seen that the sculler takes his beginning much farther behind the rigger than the oarsman, and his finish a little farther aft of the rigger.

This is due to two factors. Firstly, although there is a difference of only 1 in. (3 cm.) in the leverage of the two boats, the scull is 9 in. (23 cm.) shorter inboard than the oar—and the shorter the inboard measurement, for any given leverage, the farther the blade will swing back behind the rowlock. And secondly, the oarsman's forward reach is limited by the length of his *outside* arm. Even allowing for the fact that his outside shoulder will be stretched forward (as is shown in the sketch), the oarsman's reach, to the tip of his oar handle, is shorter than the sculler's.

A similar effect occurs at the finish of the stroke, where the sculler is able to draw both scull handles right back to his flanks, whereas the oarsman's finish is cut short at the point where his oar handle reaches his ribs on the far side of his body.

So we see that, using the same length of slide, a sculler cannot help but sweep a larger arc of water than an oarsman of the same reach. And there are two further important factors. The surface area of a pair of sculls is much greater than the surface area of an oar (see p. 35), and, unless we are comparing a double sculler with a pair, a sculling boat is moving slower than a rowing boat. So the work load, in each stroke, is greater for the sculler than for the oarsman. No doubt this is one of the reasons why sculling is a good preparation for rowing. *It is also a very good reason for not attempting to rig a sculling boat as though it were a rowing boat.*

Rowlocks and Outriggers.

It is convenient to consider the rowlock and outrigger together. The variables are fore-and-aft, vertical, lateral, and pitch.

The means of effecting adjustments vary widely. On old pattern riggers and swivels there is no provision for fore-and-aft adjustment. Lateral adjustment (moving the rowlock nearer to, or further from the centre line of boat) can be achieved by inserting wooden blocks between the outriggers and the shoulders of the boat, but only to a small extent. Vertical adjustment (the height of the rowlock above the seat) is achieved by inserting metal or leather washers beneath the top rigger stay (to lower the work), or the bottom rigger stay (to raise the work), or, if it is a single stay outrigger, welded to a single plate, underneath the top or the bottom of that plate. In other words, washers are simply used to 'tip' the outrigger up or down. It works, but on a hit or miss basis. The 'pitch', which is the inclination of the thole pin to the vertical, is the only adjustment for which provision is incorporated in the design.

More modern patterns of outriggers and rowlocks, however, have built-in provision for all these adjustments. But there are so many different methods of achieving the adjustments that I cannot attempt to describe them here, and must assume that the reader knows, or can find out, how his own equipment works.

Fore-and-aft Adjustment. We have already considered the circumstances which make it desirable for a sculler to be seated nearer to, or farther from, his 'work'. Usually this is achieved by moving the stretcher. If the outriggers provide the means of doing this, it may be regarded as an alternative to moving the stretcher. The only advantage, probably more theoretical than real, is that moving the rowlock backwards or forwards will not significantly affect the trim of the boat, as moving the stretcher will.

Height of Work. As a general rule it is desirable to have the rowlocks set as low as possible, to lower the centre of gravity. However the sculler must be able to clear the water comfortably with his blades, between the strokes. Also, at the finish of the stroke, his scull handles must come into his body between ribs and hips, and the sculler must be able to clear his thighs, with his hands, as they move away from the body in the 'recovery'.

The height of the rowlock above the seat, necessary to achieve this objective, can vary considerably, depending not only on the sculler's build, but also on his weight (which affects the level at which the boat floats), and the conditions prevailing, since rough water calls for more clearance.

The Rigging Table suggests a range of $3\frac{1}{2}$–$6\frac{1}{2}$ in. (9–17 cm.). If these extremes are exceeded it probably means that the boat is too big, or too small.

'Left-over-Right'. Because the scull handles overlap, and cross and re-cross each other during the stroke, it is usual to have one rowlock set a little higher than the other, which makes it easier for one hand to pass over the top of the other hand. This is not essential, and some scullers prefer to have one hand always a little ahead of, rather than above, the other. But a difference of about $\frac{1}{4}$ in. ($\frac{1}{2}$ cm.) is generally found to be helpful.

It does not matter which rowlock is the higher, but 'left-over-right' seems to be more common than 'right-over-left'. I suspect, but could not prove, that this is because the hand which is uppermost has a slight mechanical advantage, so that the majority of scullers, being right handed, subconsciously give the advantage to their weaker hand.

I say that it does not matter which hand is higher. But if you borrow a boat which is rigged one way, and scull the other way, you will obviously be in trouble. Also, although it is quite possible for a double sculling partnership to succeed with one member sculling left-over-right, and the other right-over-left, it looks untidy, and often results in unsteadiness. So, bearing in mind that I believe 'left-over-right' to be the more usual method, I would always recommend a beginner to try it that way first.

The Span. The span is the distance between the rowlocks, across the boat (Fig. I). On the Continent it is usually measured from the pins on which the rowlocks rotate. In Britain it is measured from the bearing surfaces of the thole pins, when the rowlock is parallel to the side of the boat. The British measurement is about $\frac{1}{3}$ in. (.85 cm.) shorter.

The span is always laterally variable, in that the boat can be fitted with longer or shorter outriggers. As already mentioned, some modern pattern outriggers are also adjustable, so that the span can be altered without taking the outriggers off the boat. With the older, conventional outriggers, the span can be increased, by a maximum of about 2 in. (5 cm.), by inserting wooden blocks between the outriggers and the side of the boat (maximum 1 in. block on each side). It cannot be shortened.

Pitch of Rowlocks. The pitch is the angle which the thole pin makes with the perpendicular. The top of the thole is normally inclined slightly towards the stern, causing the blades to be a trifle oversquared when they take the water (i.e. at the moment of entry the top of the blade will be nearer to the stern than the bottom). If the blade does not bite positively into the water, but rides up to the surface as soon as pressure is applied, then the pitch is too great. If it dives deeply into the water, then the pitch is insufficient.

Like everything else in sculling, swivel rowlock patterns vary. But the pattern illustrated in Figure VI is fairly typical, and the adjustment principle is generally the same, even though the sequence of procedure may be different. Adjustment of the pitch is made as follows:

(i) Slacken locking nut and adjusting screw.

(ii) Slacken the securing nut below the outrigger head *very slightly*.

(iii) Gently tap the adjustable plate towards the bows to increase the pitch (blade diving), or towards the stern to decrease the pitch (blade riding out).

(iv) Tighten the securing nut, adjusting screw, and locking nut, in that order.

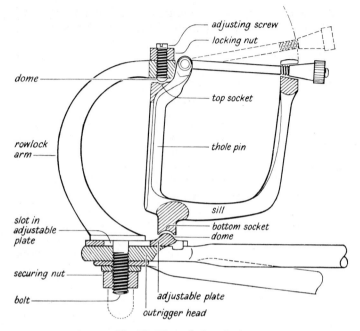

Fig. VI: The swivel rowlock

Note that the movement of the adjustable plate should be very small. If the rowlock is painted, it will be sufficient when the surface of the paint breaks. Never use a large screwdriver on the adjusting screw, as it is easy to fracture the thole pin, which is generally made of cast brass or aluminium. The adjusting screw should be tightened just sufficiently to prevent vertical play, whilst allowing the swivel to turn freely.

It is perhaps worth mentioning that the rowlock in Fig. VI is turned inwards, to point directly towards the side of the boat, for the purpose of obtaining a diagramatic view of both rowlock and outrigger head. The 'pitch', being the angle between the bearing surface of the thole pin and the perpendicular, is not apparent. In its working position the rowlock would be swung towards the reader.

An incorrect pitch is not the only thing which will cause sculls to dive, or ride up out of the water, of course. The button of the scull may be worn, the outrigger stays may be bent, or the sculler himself may be to blame. If trouble is encountered, it is as well to begin by trying another pair of sculls. If they display the same tendency to dive, or wash out, ask another sculler to try your boat, and sculls, before attempting to alter the pitch, which can be a time consuming and tricky operation. This advice, of course, is not aimed at experienced scullers, who will know well enough if their pitch is at fault.

The Sculls.

The sculls are variable as to their overall length, position of buttons, shape and size of blades, and rigidity of looms. In older pattern sculls the button was screwed to the loom (shaft) of the scull, and could therefore only be moved on the carpenter's bench, which also entailed moving the leathers. Now, however, the short leather sleeve has been replaced by a longer plastic sleeve, and the button itself is in the form of a metal collar, which can be moved up and down the shaft.

This means that it is now a simple job to shift the button, which alters the relative inboard and outboard length of the sculls. The inboard length of the scull has a dual relationship, with the span of the outriggers, and with the outboard length of the scull. This relationship, which provides the sculler's 'gearing system', is another of the key factors in sculling rigging. We shall consider this key rigging factor presently, but first we must establish the two relationships.

Inboard to Span. The inboard length of the sculls must be correct for the span, within the limits that the scull handles should overlap 8–9 in. (20–23 cm.). There are two simple formulae for calculating the correct relationships.

Where I = Inboard length of sculls, S = span, and OL = overlap of handles:—

$$\text{then } I = \frac{S}{2} + \frac{OL}{2} \quad \text{and} \quad S = I \times 2 - OL$$

If we apply the first formula, to the first column of the Rigging Table, we get:

$$I = \frac{4 \text{ ft. 9 in.}}{2} + \frac{8 \text{ in.}}{2} = \frac{65 \text{ in.}}{2} = 2 \text{ ft. } 8\tfrac{1}{2} \text{ in.}$$

or expressed metrically:

$$I = \frac{145}{2} + \frac{21}{2} = \frac{166}{2} = 83 \text{ cm.}$$

Conversely, applying the second formula to the second column of the Rigging Table, we get:

S = 2 ft. $9\tfrac{1}{4}$ in. × 2 $- 8\tfrac{1}{2}$ in. = $66\tfrac{1}{2}$ $- 8\tfrac{1}{2}$ in. = 4 ft. 10 in.
(Cm. 85 × 2 $-$ 23 = 147)

There is a margin of tolerance in applying these formulae, because the amount by which the scull handles overlap is a matter of personal preference. I have suggested a margin of one inch (3 cm.). If my formulae are applied to the championship sculling rigs quoted in the *Amateur Rowing Association Pamphlet No. 51*, published in 1970, it will be found that most fall within my suggested limits, with the exception of the USSR double, with an overlap of $7\tfrac{1}{4}$ in. (18 cm.), the West German single, with only $6\tfrac{1}{8}$ in. (15 cm.), and the

British double, with an overlap of $10\frac{3}{4}$ in. (27 cm.). In the same pamphlet, Dr. Adam's recommendations give $3\frac{1}{4}$–$7\frac{3}{4}$ in. (8–20 cm.) for singles, and $5\frac{1}{2}$–$8\frac{1}{4}$ in. (14–21 cm.) for doubles.

The objection to a small overlap is not too serious. It suggests an inadequate leverage, and may result in the hands not coming conveniently into the hips at the finish of the stroke. But both these objections can be overcome in other ways, for example by having a low O : I ratio, and by setting the stretcher to bring the sculler nearer to his work. An excessively large overlap, on the other hand, makes the handling of the sculls unnecessarily awkward, because the same gearing could be achieved without the large overlap.

Inboard to Outboard. The ratio of inboard to outboard scull lengths is, of course, not inhibited in the same way by the overlap. So long as the inboard measurement fits the span, the outboard can be as long as we like to make it. But it is this relationship which provides the sculler's gearing system. If the outboard measurement is three times as great as the inboard measurement, then the scull blade will move through an arc three times as long as the arc through which the handle moves—a gear ratio of 1 : 3.

So increasing the outboard length of the sculls makes the gearing, and therefore the work, more severe.

I have several times remarked that my rigging measurements cannot be precise, and there is perhaps no other measurement of which this is more true than the inboard: outboard relationship. One may be able to say with some confidence that a man of a particular height will need a span of a particular width. But one cannot say that a tall man will also be a strong man, requiring a severe rig, nor that a lightweight sculler will necessarily require a *pro rata* easy rig—he may be exceptionally strong for his size. Furthermore, a rig which is suitable for a sprint race may be quite unsuitable for the British Amateur Championship, sculled over a $4\frac{1}{4}$ mile course. And a rig suitable for the prevailing south-west wind, at Henley, may be too easy if there is a stiff breeze from the north.

Nevertheless it will be found that most scullers, on most occasions, work successfully with an Inboard : Outboard (I : O) ratio of between 1 : 2.42 and 1 : 2.49. These figures I calculated empirically a long time ago, and I have checked them against the scull measurements of many scullers since. If they are compared with the championship rigs quoted in the A.R.A. *Notes on Rigging*, it will be found that they generally agree, the notable exception being the 1969 British doubles partnership, which had an I.O. ratio of 1 : 2.36. Stuart Mackenzie's rigs, in the same pamphlet, also give rather low ratios, and Dr. Adams', rather high ones.

If we apply the I.O. ratios to the second column of the Rigging Table, the lower ratio gives 2 ft. $9\frac{1}{4}$ in. (33.25 in.) $\times$ 2.42 = 80.46 in., say 6 ft. $8\frac{1}{2}$ in. (205 cm.) outboard, and 9 ft. $5\frac{3}{4}$ in. (289 cm.) overall. The upper ratio gives 33.25 $\times$ 2.49 = 82.79 in., say 6 ft. $10\frac{3}{4}$ in. (211 cm.) outboard, and 9 ft. 8 in. (295 cm.) overall. So the difference between 2.42, and 2.49, in I : O ratio, allows for a difference of 2–3 in. (7 cm.) in the outboard length of an average pair of sculls.

Shape and Size of Blades. The blades of a scull are not adjustable, of course, except in so far as they can be shaved down in size, if they are found to be too large. But they come in any shape and size you care to order, or dream up. To judge by some that are seen on the river, that is what sometimes happens.

Fig. VII shows the profiles and measurements of some typical blades. Blades (a) and (c) may be described as variations of the usual standard blade in use today. I doubt whether it makes much difference whether the maximum

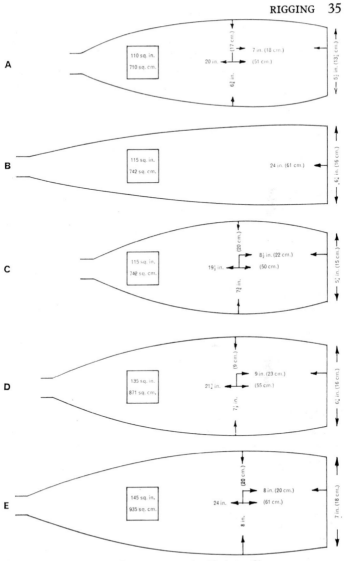

Fig. VII: Some comparative blade profiles

width is moved a little nearer to, or farther from the tip. Blade (b) is what we would now describe as the old type of blade, tapering gradually from the tip. It is, in point of fact, drawn from the measurements of one of my own 1948 Olympic sculls. One still sees such blades in use. They look like tooth picks today, but the vital statistics show that this is an optical illusion, rather than a fact.

Blade (d) is fairly typical of what some of the optimistic tigers like to use. And Blade (e) is a standard 'Macon type' **oar blade.** I have included this to illustrate the point, which I have already made, that scullers are far more severely rigged than oarsmen. Even with a pair of the smallest blades depicted in Fig. VII, the sculler would have a total blade area of 220 sq. in., compared with the 145 sq. in. of the Macon oar.

Incidentally, the areas given are 'profile' areas, not actual wetted surfaces. In other words they are taken from the flat drawings, and the actual working surface of the blade itself would be larger, depending on the curvature of the blade. As a rough guide, the surface area of my own scull, here shown as 115 sq. in., was about 125 sq. in. The shorter blades, being generally more curved, would have relatively larger wetted surface areas.

Increased curvature of the blade is reckoned to give a better grip of the water, but can also make it more difficult to extract the blades cleanly.

A glance at Blades (b) and (c) reveals another important fact. Although they have the same profile area, the working surface of (b), and the centre of thrust, is farther away from the rowlock. The mathematically minded will have no difficulty in demonstrating that this, together with the greater curvature, makes the modern blade more efficient. I readily accept this, but am not particularly impressed by the argument. For it seems to me that it is the efficiency of the sculler, not of the scull, which is of primary importance. If David had been persuaded to use the 'modern' weapons, which he was offered, he would never have killed Goliath—nor even, I suspect, if he had chosen some heavy stones to throw. But he managed very well with his smooth round pebbles. For the same reason, some of the scullers who have failed with Blade (d) might have been more successful with Blade (a) or (b).

Rigidity of the Loom. Some scullers choose stiff sculls, and some prefer them whippy. The theoretical advantage of the whippy scull is that it stores energy, during the first half of the stroke, and releases it at the finish. To achieve this the sculler's timing has to be just right, and this is not something which I could hope to describe in words.

On the other hand I am sure that rigid sculls are not desirable. The safe answer is to go to a good scull maker. But if you must make do with what is available in the boat-house, lean the sculls against the wall, with the working surface inwards, and apply pressure halfway up the loom. It should give about a couple of inches, under firm, but not excessive pressure. This is not a very scientific proposition. But if you carry out the experiment I think you will quite quickly recognise a scull which will be 'alive', but not soft.

The Working Arc. Now that we have considered the span, and the scull measurements, we can see how the relationship between span, and the inboard and outboard length of the scull, can be used to control the arc which the blade will sweep in the water.

In point of fact the blade does not 'sweep an arc' in the water at all. It would do so if we sculled a stroke in a tethered boat. But our boat, and therefore the rowlocks in which the sculls pivot, is moving through the water. But the sculls do describe an arc, *relative to the boat*, and that is sufficient for our present purpose.

It is necessary to get this arc right. It must be such that the boat is not 'pinched', by taking the beginning at too acute an angle, as much of the 'thrust' as possible must be in the desired direction (towards the stern), yet bearing in mind that a 'flatter arc' (which will produce a straighter thrust), can only be achieved by increasing the outboard length of the sculls, relative to the inboard length—and that means less leverage and therefore harder work.

The problem is illustrated in Fig. VIII. Starting with the rowlock in position R.1, and using scull S.1, the scull handle describes arc H.1, and the blade, describing arc B.1, is found to be working at too acute an angle to the boat, at both ends of the stroke (it is 'pinching'). The span is therefore increased by moving the rowlock outwards to position R.2.

The scull S.2 has the same measurements as S.1. The handle now describes arc H.2, and the blade describes arc B.2. The pinching has been eradicated, but the stroke is now short in the water, and there will almost certainly be insufficient overlap of the scull handles. This is because the inboard length of the scull is now too short for the span. So the next step is to correct the I.S. factor, by moving the button outwards. This gives us scull S.3, with the handle now describing arc H.3, which, as can be seen, is similar to the original H.1. But, as the scull is still the same length overall, increasing the inboard measurement has reduced the outboard measurement. So we have upset the I.O. factor, and the blade, now on arc B.3, is sweeping too short an arc. Finally, therefore, we restore the correct relationship between inboard and outboard measurements, by changing to scull S.4, which has the same inboard length as scull S.3, but is longer overall (and therefore outboard). Now we have the correct relationship between inboard and outboard, and also between inboard and span. The handle is describing arc H.3, and the blade is describing arc B.4.

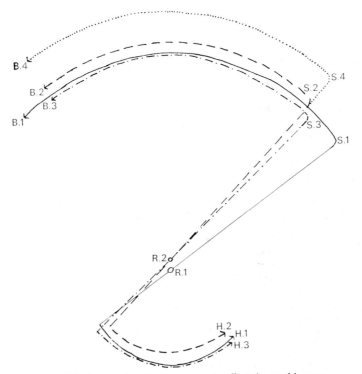

Fig. VIII: Span and scull measurements affect the working arc

In practice it is not necessary to work through all these steps, of course. Having decided that we need a wider span, we know, from the I.S. and I.O. formulae, what the measurements of the scull will have to be.

If we now turn back to Fig. IV, we remember that we concluded that, if adjustment to the stretcher failed to achieve a comfortable and strong position, at both ends of the stroke, the solution would have to be sought elsewhere. *The I.O. and I.S. formulae give us that solution.*

By a combination of adjustments to the stretcher, to the span, and to the inboard and outboard length of the sculls, we can now arrange for a man of any size to scull any length of stroke, sweeping through any arc we wish. By the same method, coupled with the choice of the appropriate size and shape of blade, we can, furthermore, arrange that, for a given output of work, the stroke through the water will be completed in a particular period of time.

In terms of a single sculler, this means that we can select a rig to suit a particular rate of striking. In terms of double sculling it means that, even if we have two men of different size and strength, we can rig them so that their blades will remain parallel throughout the stroke, and that both will take the same time to complete a stroke, even though one is stronger than the other.

How to use Rigging. We have now completed our survey of rigging. We have seen what the variables are, and their effects. And, from the Rigging Table, we have the basic measurements, which are likely to suit an average sculler on most occasions.

How is this knowledge to be used?

There is no simple answer to this question, because, as I have already pointed out, I cannot write for an individual sculler, in individual circumstances. The circumstances are changing all the time, and one hopes that the sculler is too—for the better.

The Rigging Table provides a point of departure. But rigging is a continuing process, like the acquisition of technique, which I shall discuss in the next chapter. The mere process of improvement calls for change, and so, of course, do varying conditions. This does not mean that it is a good idea to be continually fiddling with the rigging. But it does mean that you cannot rig a boat correctly on 1st September, and forget about it until the end of the following summer.

The fact that the rigs of some of the world's leading scullers differ considerably from some of my recommended measurements, does not mean that they are wrong, or that my advice is wrong. It is, on the contrary, a confirmation of what I have just said. But it emphatically does not mean that the club sculler has only to adopt a 'Demiddi rig', or a 'Malischev rig', to enter world-class competition. The reverse is true.

So, if there is an answer to the question, 'How do we use rigging?', it is to start from the safe base provided by the Rigging Table, and to progress cautiously, according to the advice in this chapter. And remember that it is better to make one adjustment at a time, rather than several together, which will only obscure the effect of the change.

II

TECHNIQUE

SCULLING IS A PRECISE TECHNICAL OPERATION. It is difficult to think of any other sporting activity which calls for such a complex series of movements, and the inter-action and co-ordination of so many different muscle groups.

Not all successful scullers look alike, of course. They develop individual styles, and if they are successful we can hardly say that they are wrong, though some succeed by brute force, and perhaps could have been better still if they had also been more skilful. But, basically, nearly all good scullers are good because their technique is good. Certainly those lower down the scale are most likely to progress if they pay attention to technique.

It is difficult to describe sculling technique in writing, because sculling is a continuous, flowing action, and one can only describe it, in writing, by describing a series of separate points. But there is no other way.

Basic Positions.

Remember that the basic positions in sculling are not static, though they are necessarily described as such. They are important because correct positions lead to correct movements.

The Feet. The correct position for the feet on the stretcher is the same as the position in which you would naturally place your feet on the floor to do a 'deep-knees-bend' exercise. This is not surprising, as the movement of sliding forward in a sculling boat is similar to doing a 'deep-knees-bend' sitting down.

The heels should be an inch or two apart, with the feet splayed at an angle of about 25 degrees. This provides a firm base on the stretcher, just as it does on the floor.

The Knees. At the beginning of the stroke the knees should be opened to approximately the width apart of the armpits. A man with a short body and long legs may need to open the knees a little wider, to get his full reach between them. A man with short legs and a long body may hold them a trifle closer, and swing over them. But the knees should never be closed, nor should they 'flop' apart. And, of course, they must always be symmetrical.

Sitting Position. The sculler should sit squarely on the bones of his posterior, with his weight evenly distributed. He should sit up to his full height, like an alert spectator at an exciting football match. The back should therefore be straight, but not stiff.

The Head. If the eyes look out level from the head, focussed on a point about 30 yards astern, the head will naturally maintain its proper angle with the body. At the catch the chin will be slightly raised, and at the finish, lowered. The neck should be firm but relaxed, and the head must never be allowed to loll sideways, nor to fall forward onto the chest.

Hands and Wrists. The correct hold of the sculls (note—not *grip*) is of paramount importance. The scull handle is held between the roots of the fingers and the fingers themselves, not in the palm of the hand. The thumb must always remain over the end of the handle, exerting a light pressure outwards against the button, never wrapped underneath the handle.

Basic Movements.

The Legs. There have been many arguments as to whether the legs should be regarded as a *primary* or a *secondary* source of power, or, if you like to put this very unscientifically, whether they are directly propelling the boat, using the body and arms as connecting links, or simply propelling the body, from its optimum position for taking the catch, to its optimum position for taking the finish.

The argument itself may be academic, but it is useful if it helps us to assess what the legs have to do.

Of course the legs do propel the boat. If you hold your blades square in the water, and push with the legs, without swinging the body back or bending the arms, the boat will move forward. And of course the legs also propel the body, from the front stop to the back stop.

The problem is that these two functions are antagonistic. For the legs can drive the body back much faster if the body leaves the sculls behind—and this is precisely what they will do, if given the chance.

To be effective, therefore, *the power of the legs must be countered by the muscles of the lower back and loins, which must try not to be driven back towards the backstop. By resisting the legs, this diverts the thrust, upwards, through the body, to the sculls.*

So, during the stroke, the legs must thrust steadily, but not explosively, backwards. They must work symmetrically, with the same thrust applied through each leg, and the knees moving down together. Ideally this movement should last almost to the finish of the stroke, and, generally speaking, the better the sculler the more nearly will he achieve this co-ordination of legs and slide.

At the finish the knees should be pressed down firmly, and should remain so until the body swings forward, through the perpendicular, towards the next stroke. As the sculler slides forward it is important that the knees rise, and open, symmetrically, maintaining equal pressure with both feet against the stretcher.

Swing from the Hips. The use of long slides has largely replaced the long swing which used to be fashionable. Nevertheless there is always a considerable element of 'swing' from the hips in a sculler's movement. Here is a good example of how a correct *position* will lead to a correct *movement*. For if the sculler is sitting up at the finish, with a strong back, and his weight evenly distributed on his seat, he will naturally *swing* forward from his hips, on the centre line of the boat. What is more, his weight will at once be transferred to his stretcher, making for good balance. But if he is slumped on his seat like an effigy of Buddha, he will roll forward like an ungainly fat man struggling out of a deck chair.

We call this movement the 'recovery', and its timing is important. The hands should lead the shoulders forward, as though the sculls were pulling the sculler forward, rather than being pushed forward by him. As the top half of the body swings forward, the weight is transferred from the back to the front of the seat, and as it moves through the perpendicular, but not before, the knees relax and begin to rise. The weight must be in front of the slide, and sliding and swinging must be co-ordinated during the forward movement, just as they were during the working part of the stroke.

The most common faults here are, (i) swinging forward too far, too soon, so that the shoulders are forced to lift to avoid the knees as the sculler approaches the front stop, and (ii) delaying the swing, which leads to 'diving' over the stretcher.

The Shoulders. The Correct action of the shoulders, at the finish of the stroke, is the same as the action in 'Rolling the Shoulders', with or without weights. The shoulders are drawn upwards, backwards (as far as possible), and downwards. Steve Fairbairn used to describe it as 'turning mother's mangle', and he was not far wrong.

Note that this is another movement which cannot be made correctly unless the body is in the correct position. In Figure IV our friend 'A' could not possibly roll his shoulders back, because his hands are cramped in his stomach, so that he cannot even draw his elbows back, and 'C' cannot do it for the opposite reason—his scull handles are too far away.

The Arms. At the catch the arms should be relaxed, and straight. Some people find it more natural to have slightly flexed arms, and this is acceptable. But it is not acceptable to try to 'take the beginning' with the arms—'snatching' as we sometimes call it. This fault is usually caused by the sculler being heavy-handed and slow on the catch—his legs do not spring his body back quickly enough, and he tries to remedy this by snatching with his arms.

The arms should begin to flex naturally, about a third of the way through the stroke, and their contribution to the propulsion of the boat follows this, building up to a maximum draw at the finish. Once the slide has reached the backstop, and the body has completed its backward swing, the sculler really has only his arms left. And, at the end of the working stroke, this is the moment when the boat must be accelerating to its fastest speed. So it is really necessary to have the power of the arms at this point. Furthermore, the whippy strength of the arms is good for this accelerating action, but not at all good for taking the sudden, heavy weight, at the beginning of the stroke.

If the arms tire excessively, or suffer from cramp, it is nearly always due, either to snatching at the beginning, or to gripping the scull handles too tightly.

At the finish the arms will move correctly if the shoulders move correctly. The elbows should be close to the flanks, but not constricted, and the arms should be drawing straight back, not outwards from the body. If the sculler is rigged too far from his work (Fig. IV 'C') he will find his scull handles moving apart at the finish, instead of coming in below his ribs, and will be unable to get this 'backward' draw.

As the sculls are extracted, the arms drop to provide clearance, and are immediately, but not violently, straightened, to commence 'leading' the body forwards again. The recovery has been likened to a billiard ball bouncing off the cushion. It is not an entirely happy comparison, for there must be no 'bounce' at the finish. But the smooth resilience, with which the cushion of a good billiard table reverses the direction of the ball, does suggest the way in which the hands and arms come into, and away from the body, without check or hurry.

Hands and Wrists. Try this experiment with a length of thick piping, or a round pole resting on the backs of two chairs, so that it is free to rotate. Place the tips of the fingers on the pole, and rotate it by rolling the fingers away from you, keeping them in close contact with the pole. The top joints of the fingers will disappear 'over the horizon', followed by the middle joints, the wrist will rise slightly, and the crook of the thumb will come into contact with the underside of the pole. This is the movement of hand and wrist in squaring the blade, prior to taking the catch.

Rowing coaches sometimes speak of 'raising the hands' to put the blades into the water, but it may be better to think in terms of spring off the stretcher, which causes the body to rise, putting the blades into the water. The position of the hands and wrists does not change until the arms bend, when the wrists begin to rise. The 'arching' of the wrist increases as the hands come in to the finish, not because there is any deliberate raising of the wrists, but because, as the elbows bend, the forearm drops, increasing the angle with the wrist.

At the finish of the stroke the rotation of the shoulders 'unrolls' the wrist again. If you return to the pole, which we used to demonstrate the beginning of the stroke, and now roll it back towards your body, letting the fingers uncoil, you have the finishing movement of hands and wrists.

This movement, with a downward pressure on the scull handles, extracts and feathers the blades. The wrists are then dropped, and the scull handles lie, not in the palm of the hand, but beneath the roots of the fingers. Immediately, the hands move away from the body, clearing the thighs, and begin to lead the body forward to the next stroke.

This sequence is probably the most difficult of all sculling movements to describe. Hopefully the photographs in Chapter III will fill in the gaps.

Remember that the scull handles should never be gripped tightly, and that they are held by the fingers, and the roots of the fingers, rather than by the palms. In practice it is unusual to have the sculls knocked out of the hands, even in rough water. But it is important that the rubber grips should always be in good condition, with plenty of 'tread'. For racing, and particularly in wet weather, or hot weather when excessive sweating is likely, it is advisable to rub a little powdered rosin on the hands. This does not last indefinitely, so take a little in a matchbox, in the bottom of the boat, and apply it just before the start.

The Continuous Cycle.

I have now tried to describe the basic positions and movements in sculling. But sculling, as we have already pointed out, is not a series of positions or movements, but a live and fluid cycle. In training, the sculler must direct his attention to a succession of details, but never forgetting that it is the continuous cycle which matters.

Coming Forward. When we talk of the 'beginning' and

'finish' of the stroke we are really referring only to the pro-
pulsive part of the cycle. In considering the complete cycle
it is more convenient to begin from the backstop, whence,
having completed one stroke, the sculler moves forward into
the next.

So long as the hands 'lead' the body away from the backstop, the swing is likely to follow correctly. The knees should
be held down as the body swings through the perpendicular,
but should not be held down artificially after this. The blades
should be well clear of the water during the forward swing,
and should remain feathered as long as possible, to reduce
wind resistance. As the sculler approaches the frontstop, he
should get the impression that his hands are rising up in front
of him. They do not really rise, until the blades are squared
for the catch, but they seem to do so, relative to the movement of the shoulders.

Traditional teaching used to be that the recovery, and
initial swing forward from the back stop, should be executed
quickly, and that the pace of the slide should slow down as
it approaches the front stop. We have seen variations over
the years, including a deliberate check at the finish and
acceleration towards the front stop. My personal belief is
that the speed of the boat through the water dictates the pace
at which the sculler slides forward. He should let the boat
freely carry him out, but always retaining control, through
the pressure of his feet on the stretcher.

The Stroke in the Water. If you sit at your frontstop
in a stationary boat, with blades flat on the water (or in the
air, if your balance is good enough), and then drive with the
legs, the boat will move backwards. This is because the
sculler, and his boat, together constitutes a 'mechanical
system', of which the sculler is by far the heavier part. If the
sculler moves in one direction, the rest of the system (i.e.
the boat), will move in the opposite direction, if it is free to
do so. Only when the system as a whole has created a point

of resistance, outside itself, can it be moved in the desired direction.

This resistance is supplied by the action of the blades in the water. But water itself has inconvenient properties. You can submerge your hand and move it slowly, without experiencing any significant resistance. But if you try to move your hand very fast, the resistance will be so great that you may be unable to keep it submerged. And if you take a swipe at the water, from above the surface, you will just create a big splash.

These two factors together create the problem in taking the beginning in sculling. The whole system is moving past the water. To create further propulsion the blades must 'catch up' with the water, and impart movement to it. If they are too slow they will 'back-water' the boat, instead of propelling it forward. If they are too fast they will bounce off the surface. And to move them at all, the sculler has got to reverse his own direction of movement, relative to the boat.

The solution to this problem cannot be reduced to words, but must be learned by experience. It is a problem of coordinating the thrust of the legs against the stretcher, the springing back of the body, and the burying of the blades in the water. The indicators to watch are the blades at the moment of entry, and the stern of the boat. If the blades are moving too slowly they will create 'back-splash', towards the bows. If they are moving too fast they will create splash towards the stern. If they are moving at just the right speed, they will create exactly the same splash as if you drop them squarely into the water, when the boat is stationary—just a few drops from both front and back surfaces.

A moving boat cannot avoid creating some turbulence in the water. Correct timing of the spring at the beginning of the stroke minimises stern turbulence. An observer on the bank will be able to note the amount of check on the forward run of the boat. But the sculler himself cannot see this, and can only judge by his stern wave.

Having taken his beginning, the sculler must then try to accelerate all the way to the finish. *The pressure must increase, because the moment it slacks off, the resistance of the water to the working surface of the blades will disappear.* In an extreme case, if the blades actually decelerate, they will, of course, begin to back-water, and positively stop the boat.

If you reflect that the blades are in the water for less than half the time taken for the complete stroke cycle, which means that the boat has got to keep on running, without propulsion, the truth of the old cry that 'races are won between the strokes' is very apparent.

And so we have reached the moment of truth, which is that *the sculler's task is to impart maximum speed to the boat at the* **finish of the stroke.**

Only the spring from the stretcher can move the blades fast enough to catch the water at the beginning of the stroke. Only if the back is held firm can the thrust of the legs be transmitted to the blades. Once legs and back muscles are fully committed, only the draw of the arms can impart the necessary acceleration of the blades, towards the finish of the stroke.

Some experienced scullers gain power at the finish by 'pulling up' the body on the scull handles. This is not wrong, but it is not a practice I would recommend to those who are not experienced. If a sculler is visibly pulling up his body, at the finish, he is almost certainly overdoing it, and you will probably also be able to see that he is 'bouncing' his boat in the process.

Balance. In some ways balance should perhaps have come at the beginning of this chapter, for no one can scull well until he is comfortable and confident, and no one can be comfortable and confident without good balance.

Balance is theoretically more difficult in a sculling boat than in a rowing boat, because sculls are shorter than oars (the longer the pole which a tight-rope walker uses, the more secure is his balance). But a sculler has the advantage, over the oarsman, that he is handling the sculls on both sides of his boat, and knows that nobody else is upsetting him.

It is possible to prevent a sculling boat from rolling by allowing the blades to brush lightly on the surface of the water, and most scullers do this, to a greater or less extent. But this practice is, in effect, concealing the causes of imbalance, whereas the Complete Sculler must aim to achieve positive balance.

An empty sculling boat should balance itself on an even keel. So unsteadiness can only be caused by outside agencies —the water, the wind, or the sculler himself. It often is caused by wind and water. But there is no future in giving up as a bad job, on that account, because, when it comes to a race, it is the sculler who is most skilful at countering these inconveniences who will benefit. The world's best golfers will devote many hours to practising a single shot. The same is true of billiards and tennis players. A cricketer, or a jumper, may have to take infinite pains over such an apparently simple problem as how many paces he must take, and how long they must be, to bring him to the bowling crease, or the take-off board, at the optimum moment. Yet many scullers, even in the higher echelons, imagine that good balance will simply 'happen', if they go on sculling for long enough. That is precisely what it will not do, unless they take the trouble to find out what *they* are doing to cause imbalance, and to correct it.

A boat will roll if anything is done on either side of its centre line, which is not exactly balanced on the other side.

The sculler can only 'do things' to his boat at the points at which he is in contact with the boat. There are only three such points:—

   (i) *The feet are in contact with the stretcher.* So the pressure on each foot must be equal at all times.

  (ii) *The body is in contact with the seat,* and the centre of the seat is on the centre line of the boat. Therefore the sculler's weight must be equally distributed on both buttocks, the body must move straight up and down the centre line of the boat, and the legs must move symmetrically on both sides of the centre line.

 (iii) *The hands are in contact with the sculls,* which rest in the rowlocks. This is the most sensitive point of contact, because the rowlocks are far from the centre line. Raising or lowering a hand varies the downward pressure on the rowlocks, whether the blades are in the air, or the water. Also the outward pressure, which must be exerted by the thumbs, to keep the scull buttons pressed against the thole pins, has the effect of transferring weight to the sill of the rowlock. So, too, will any increase in the pull exerted against the thole pin during the stroke.

The forces applied at all these suspension points are acting on the balance of the boat at all times. Balance, or lack of balance, is a combination of them all. However experienced the sculler, he should devote a few minutes, once or twice during every outing, to consciously and methodically checking through the three suspension points. It is best to do this in stages. First scull ten strokes, concentrating on the feet on the stretcher, then ten strokes checking that the swing is straight, the weight evenly distributed on both buttocks, and the knees symmetrical, and a final ten strokes concentrating on the hands, and the forces which they are applying to the rowlocks.

Methodical Practice. It is not only balance which calls for *methodical* practice, though this happens to be an easy example to illustrate in words. All the factors discussed in this chapter need to be learned, and perfected by practice.

Presumably nobody goes on sculling, year after year, without some natural ability, and a considerable love of the sport. So there must be something wrong with a sculler's technique, if he does not improve. If he wants to improve, he must find out what is wrong, and then put it right. The oarsman should be able to rely on the coach. But the sculler gets very little coaching. Therefore he must search out his faults for himself, and set about correcting them, one by one. To achieve this he must plan a programme, for every outing, for every week, and for every month, and consciously and methodically work at each point in turn. As I have repeatedly said, *it is no good 'just going on sculling and hoping that it will come right'.* **It will only come right if you put it right.**

III

SEEING CRITICALLY

All of us see hundreds and maybe thousands of scullers every year. But how critically do we look at them, and do we remember, and learn from what we see? Sculling is of the mind as well as of the body. It is the mind that directs the body and it is the 'mind's eye' which receives the signals. Not every sculler who is winning a race is necessarily sculling well – he may be stronger or more determined than his opponents. And the converse is equally true. So 'seeing critically' is a worthwhile exercise.

It is not easy to take in and analyze all that we see when watching scullers in action. Photography gives us a second chance, and in some respects a better chance. In this book all the photographs are concentrated in this chapter, rather than being spread throughout the text. Hopefully this gives them more impact and certainly it makes comparisons easier. There are as many lessons to be learned here as in the whole of the preceding chapter. And they are the same lessons, of course. I have refrained from making textual references to the photographs elsewhere in the book so that there should be no break in the continuity and concentration of reading. Now is the time for those who have read the text so far, to seek out the lessons for themselves.

Plate 1 shows Joachim Dreifke of the German Democratic Republic (GDR), dominant in single, double, and quadruple sculls during the decade 1974–1984. Dreifke was a muscular

Plate 1 Joachim Dreifke – Explosive Power

sculler, but note the relaxed arms and arched wrist at the catch. Here we see the unleashing of explosive power under total control.

We can see the same sort of power from two less muscular men, Great Britain's Mike Hart and Chris Baillieu, in Plate 2. The purist might say that Baillieu's back was less firm than Hart's, and that this has allowed the legs to move the slide back a trifle too fast. But Baillieu, who has described himself as 'more of a heavy lightweight than a heavyweight' always had to rely on fierce attack to make up for lack of body weight. Mike Hart's position here is hard to fault.

Plate 3 is of myself and Bert Bushnell shortly before the Olympic Regatta in 1948. When you have got over laughing at the antique blades (and checked the blade profiles in Fig. VII), this picture has relevance to Chapter V, as an example of how two men differing nearly six inches in height and 3 stone (19 kg.) in weight, can be rigged to form an effective partnership. To the modern eye the body swing must look exaggerated. We used fixed stretchers and were sliding level with the work. Bushnell used sculls 9 ft. 9 in. (297.2 cm.)

Plate 2 M. J. Hart and C. L. Baillieu

overall and 2 ft. 9½ in. (85.1 cm.) inboard, on a span of 4 ft. 11 in. (149.8 cm.), whilst my sculls were 9 ft. 10 in. (299.7 cm.) overall, 2 ft. 10½ in. (87.6 cm.) inboard, on a span of 5 ft, ¼ in. (153 cm.).

Plate 3 B. H. T. Bushnell and R. D. Burnell

I am conscious that Plate 4, besides being a less than perfect reproduction, is an uncharitable view of Mervyn Wood, here seen with M. T. Riley in 1958, ten years after Wood's Olympic success. If Wood's reputation were not secure in the halls of fame I would hesitate to publish this picture, taken long after his heyday. But I would like you to look back at Fig. IV in Chapter I. Here is 'Mr. C' in real life, too far back from his scull handles to hold onto his finish.

Plate 4 M. T. Riley and M. Wood

Plate 5 shows Dreifke again, this time in mid-stroke. In fact it is beyond mid-stroke to judge by the position of his left scull. Note that his body has already swung through the perpendicular so that his weight is truly hung onto his blades, demonstrating the strength of his back, which has resisted the leg drive. The knees are not yet flattened and the arms are only just beginning to break, in preparation for the powerful draw which will surely accelerate his boat at the finish of the stroke.

The sequence shown in Plates 6–10 features Pertti Karpinnen, the 'Flying Finn,' who was probably as near to 'The Complete Sculler' as we are likely to see. Tall and lean,

Plate 5 Joachim Dreifke – A Strong Back

Karpinnen was blessed with perfect physique and might be described as the 'Gentle Giant' of sculling. Plates 6 and 7 show how he caresses his sculls into the water; the awesome power of his leg drive is seen in Plates 8 and 9 – but the slide goes with the legs, never ahead; and the sequence ends (Plate 10) as it began, in repose, as he allows his boat to run away from the finish. Perhaps I allow my enthusiasm to run away with my pen, but for me Karpinnen's sculling was special.

The sequence of Christine Scheiblich (GDR) in Plates 11–14 proves the old adage that there is an exception to every rule. Scheiblich was among the best, and certainly among the most successful women scullers we have seen. Plate 11 shows a perfect gather over the stretcher, leading to a well timed catch (Plate 12). But compare Plates 13 and 14 with Karpinnen's Plates 8 and 9. Scheiblich's leg drive seems to have

Plates 6–10 Pertti Karpinnen

Plates 11 — 14 Christine Scheiblich

overcome the resistance of her back, so that her slide reaches the back stop (perhaps we should say 'the end of its journey' as she probably used no working back stop) when the stroke is still only half way to completion. In a lesser sculler one would predict a weak finish, but it hardly looks like it in Plate 14. Her arms and shoulders must surely have been phenomenally strong. Readers must form their own conclusions. Scheiblich's reputation is not at risk from my criticism.

Plate 15 shows Dreifke again, here stroking the East German quad in Bled in 1979. I offer this as a fun picture for the benefit of coaches who we sometimes hear exhorting their pupils to 'follow stroke.' Human reactions being what they are, 'following stroke' is not quite good enough, is it? But at this level of competition who is going to quibble about a hundredth part of a second – except perhaps the finishing judge? Or perhaps Dreifke, who must have felt the weight of the boat before bow's blade was finally covered.

Plate 15 GDR Quad – Following Stroke

Plate 16 Alf and Frank Hansen

Finally we come to Norway's Hansen brothers, Frank and Alf, and I suppose there has never been any crew or sculler quite so dominant in any event, for so long. Perhaps Plate 16 tells us why. This is another photograph which is taken from an action sequence, so there is no question of posing. This really is the world's finest double at speed. When you can time your beginning so precisely to the pace of the boat, so that the blades break the surface almost without disturbing the water, then indeed you are well on the way to becoming 'The Complete Sculler.'

IV

SCULLING FOR ROWING

I GAVE THE TITLE, *Sculling for Rowing*, to my last book, because it was specifically aimed at those who were suddenly required to prove their worth, as oarsmen, by beating other people at sculling.

Actually I went to Oxford one day, hopefully to watch the university crew in training, and found its aspirant members, in an odd assortment of boats, sculling unmeasured distances, without supervision. This seemed to me to be a rather unprofitable method of preparing for the Boat Race. Of course it was not the way it was intended to be done. But I concluded that, if oarsmen all over the country were going to be introduced to sculling, by coaches, many of whom had probably never done any, it must be worthwhile to offer them at least some rudimentary advice.

There is nothing new in this world, and some discerning coaches have long appreciated that a successful sculler is a useful man to have in a crew. This should be self-evident, for a sculler succeeds or fails by his own unaided efforts. But the practice of actually selecting crews on the results of sculling trials between the candidates, is ascribed to Dr. Karl Adams, of Ratzburg.

Of course those who thought about it, no doubt including Dr. Adams, soon recognised the flaws in this method of selection. It can be quite effective as applied to complete beginners, since, starting from scratch, those who make the most rapid progress in sculling boats are generally those with the greatest aptitude for rowing. But with more or less adult oarsmen, to put it bluntly, some are already experienced scullers and some are not. And the objection goes deeper than that. For there are undoubtedly men who are excellent value, in an eight, as *followers*, but who are mentally incapable of driving themselves in a sculling boat.

However that may be, many British coaches, who have become past-masters at borrowing other people's ideas without applying any original thought, continue the practice of sculling selection. And, even if it does not produce the best crews, it still has some beneficial side effects. For one thing, it results in clubs spending money on sculling boats. Also it introduces new men to sculling, and some become good scullers, whilst some idle and ineffectual oarsmen may be unmasked. And some coaches, of course, are constrained to learn more about sculling.

From the coach's point of view, sculling is a useful adjunct to rowing, whether it is used as a primary means of selection or not. It teaches and reveals watermanship, for the sculler must balance his own boat, and if he is unable to do so it is at least an indication that he may also be contributing to unsteadiness in the eight. By the same token, it also reveals characteristics of determination, courage, competitiveness, and so on.

Strictly from the rowing point of view, these attributes can be developed just as well, and perhaps better, in a pair. But even in a two-man boat the conclusions will not be quite so clear, since either member of the partnership may be responsible for either good or bad results.

So, in spite of some criticism of the way it has been used, I am not suggesting that 'sculling for rowing' is not to be recommended. I am sure that it is, providing its limitations are recognised. I have only one further word for the rowing coach, therefore. Let him please remember that, if he is going to send his men out sculling, and in any way judge them by the results, he has a duty to see that they are properly rigged and supervised. Which means, of course, that he must do his homework conscientiously, and become a sculling coach as well as a rowing coach.

From the pupil's point of view, the problem is less complisated. Whether or not his primary objective is to become a sculler, he has everything to gain, and nothing to lose, by learning to scull as well as he can.

If he is being asked to scull as part of his training programme for rowing, it is certain that he will be judged be results to some extent. As the present tendency is to pick the strongest available men for a crew, even if they are not the most skilful, and as all of them, being in the same squad, are likely to be carrying out the same programme of physicly training, it follows that the man who can acquire the most tkill as a sculler is likely to prevail. Which is, after all, the object of the exercise, and the best possible reason for studying this book.

V

DOUBLE AND QUADRUPLE SCULLING

IT IS STILL UNFORTUNATELY TRUE, as I wrote in *The Oxford Pocket Book of Sculling Training*, in 1962, that double sculling has been slow to progress in popularity in Britain. I think the reason for this remains the same as it was ten years ago—that is, a shortage of boats. The single shell has become an essential item in club equipment. The double has not. And when an individual sculler decides to buy himself a boat, that will almost certainly be a single, too. The club is only constrained to invest in a double when it has a partnership of considerable promise—and how are two men to show considerable promise in a double, when they have no boat to scull in? It is a vicious circle.

This is a pity, for double sculling is a rewarding class of boat, and although the standard is high at the top, as it is in all classes, it is less demanding, at the present time, than single sculling. With the large number of men who have been introduced to sculling, as part of their training for rowing, double sculling should be capable of a boom, if only the boats were available.

There is no significant difference in the technique of single and double sculling, though the fact that the double moves faster calls for rather more finesse and quickness. The key to successful doubling is togetherness. And the key to togetherness lies in rigging. All coaches must be well aware that the two men in a double must take the catch, and the finish, together, and remain in phase throughout the stroke. Yet one frequently sees double partnerships in which the bow and the stroke men are hopelessly out of phase.

All the information necessary to rig a double sculler is in Chapter I. The only new problem is that, in addition to being individually rigged comfortably and efficiently, the two men must now also be rigged so that their blades enter and leave the water parallel, and take the same time to complete the stroke.

If the two partners are similar in build and strength, their rigging requirements may be identical, and there will be no problem. But if one has a longer reach than the other he will probably need a wider span, and longer sculls, so that the two sets of sculls shall work parallel to each other. A glance back at Figure VIII shows how this can be achieved.

But there is another factor to consider. Both men must also take the same length of time to complete the stroke. If one is stronger than the other, and if they both sweep the same arc of water, then the stronger man is likely to finish ahead of the weaker man. To prevent this he can either be given larger blades, or his sculls can be relatively longer outboard, so that, although they continue to move through the same angle, his blades will describe a longer arc in the water.

So the relevant rigging factors are:—

  (i) the position of the stretcher, which moves the sculler forward or backward in the boat;

 (ii) the width of the span and the inboard length of the sculls, which decides the angle through which the sculls will turn;

(iii) the outboard length of the sculls, which determines the length of the arc of the water swept;

(iv) the size of the blades, which, together with the arc swept, controls the work-load in a given stroke.

The combination of all these factors is infinitely variable. So, in theory at least, it should be possible to have a short, thick-set man, of great strength, sliding well up to his work, using a narrow span and short sculls with a high outboard-inboard ratio, and wide blades, partnered by a tall thin man, who is relatively weak, stopped back from his work, using a wide span with long sculls, low outboard-inboard ratio, and small blades, and still to have them perfectly together.

To achieve harmony in such an ill-assorted partnership might be quite a complicated task. But it will not very often be necessary!

There is one other minor point to consider in rigging a double. We have noted elsewhere that, to cater for the fact that his scull handles cross and re-cross, during every stroke, the sculler usually works with one hand 'above', or 'leading', the other. In a double it is desirable that both men should solve this problem in the same way, both men sculling 'left-over-right', or *vice versa*, or both leading with the same hand. This is not absolutely essential, but where the partners differ in this respect, it does sometimes adversely affect their timing and balance.

Quadruple Sculling. Quadruple sculling will make its international début in the World Championships in 1974, so that an increasing interest in this new class is to be expected. No doubt a shortage of boats will limit its popularity in some countries. But, as a 'quad' will essentially be a club crew, rather than a venture for individuals, the cost of boats may turn out to be less of a handicap than in the case of doubles.

I have never sculled in a quad, but I have sculled, recrea-tionally, in an octuple. This certainly does not make me an expert. But few of those concerned with the new class will be experts, initially.

I do not think that quads will introduce any new rigging problems. It is more likely that what I have just said about doubles will apply equally to quads. The most obvious difference will be that quadruple scullers will be exceedingly fast boats, probably as fast as eights, though perhaps unable to maintain this speed over the full distance. It seems likely that we shall need a higher outboard-inboard ratio, to provide the gearing needed to take the catch without excessive slip. This will be not so much a new problem, as a new emphasis on an old problem. Those who understand rigging should be able to cope with it.

VI

TRAINING

THE RAW MATERIALS OF SUCCESS are the boat, the technique, and the man himself. We have dealt with the boat, and tried to describe the technique. Now we have to consider how the man is going to prepare himself, physically and mentally, to make the best possible use of his boat and technique, when the moment comes to race. This is 'training'.

Many people, today, would say that training is more important than technique and rigging. I will only repeat that the Complete Sculler must 'have it all'.

Let us then assume a sculler who has already acquired a sound technique, or is in process of doing so, and who has a suitable boat, properly rigged, and sufficient understanding of rigging to enable him to adjust his equipment as circumstances may demand (and they will, as conditions change and his own performance improves). Now, at this moment in time, he decides that he is going for 'the big league'. How should he set about it?

Planning. The first step is to work out a plan of campaign. Far too many scullers, even in Elite class, go on, year after year, without ever showing any real improvement. I am sure this is because they fail to plan, beyond perhaps deciding 'to start a little earlier and work a little harder, next year'. This is simply 'serving up the mixture as before'. If they have 'done a bit more work', the odds are that their opponents have done likewise.

What they need is:

(i) A plan for increasing their physical potential.

(ii) A plan for developing their technical ability towards its highest potential.

(iii) A plan for the racing season itself, to ensure that they can produce their peak performance when it is actually needed.

It would be helpful if I could forthwith offer a draft programme for achieving these objectives. A good coach, knowing his pupils and their circumstances, should do just this. But all I know is that every sculler is an individual, with individual problems. One may be a student, with academic hours, and commitments, and three vacation periods each year, during which he may or may not have to work to earn some pocket money. Another may be a 9—5 office worker, short of exercise but full of energy. And yet another may be what the A.R.A. rules used to describe as a 'manual labourer', bulging with muscle but exhausted at the end of the day.

It is impractical to offer a year's programme applicable to everyone, and, I think, unrealistic to offer an 'ideal programme' for the fortunate man who has nothing else to do. So I offer no programmes.

Each individual must work out his own programme, unless he is a member of an organised squad, when it will be done for him—or at least so one hopes. He should not regard this as a troublesome chore, because *preparing a training programme is part of the preparation for becoming a Complete Sculler*. It requires him to take stock of his present assets and defects, and to think deeply about his objectives, and how to achieve them. The mere act of thinking about it will start him off on the right road.

Of course it is not reasonable to sit down in September and plan exactly what you intend to do on the river on the 5th July (unless 5th July happens to be the final day of next year's Henley Regatta). But at least you can make your appreciation of what is necessary, and plan your long term strategy. Also you can plan the details of your winter campaign. Later, after Christmas, you can plan for the spring. And later still, to complete the military analogy, you can plan your battles before each regatta.

Planning must be flexible, to allow for bad weather, ills and ailments, family commitments, and so on. But try to keep within the planned framework, and never start a training session, whether on the water or on dry land, without knowing exactly what you are going to do. *The act of thinking about what you are going to do makes it more likely that you will do it well.*

Successful sculling is not just a function of the arms and legs, or even of heart and lungs. It is also a function of the brain.

The brain needs training just as much as the body does, and the result is even more important, since the brain has to direct the body. From this it follows that the sculler's training is not to be confined to a couple of hours work-out in the boat, or gymnasium. It can usefully continue throughout his waking hours, and perhaps during his sleeping hours as well. When you catch yourself unconsciously controlling your breathing, as you walk to the office, practising wrist exercises as you compose a letter, and thinking about your next opponent when you wake up in the morning, you will know that you are on the right track.

Planning a Programme. What is it, then, that you have to plan for?

The sculler's training requirements fall into three categories:

1. Technique.

2. Physical potential, which can be sub-divided into:
   (a) Strength
   (b) Stamina
   (c) Wind
   (d) General health, including feeding.

3. Preparations for racing.

The current tendency is to emphasise physical potential, rather than technical potential. There are several reasons for this.

Firstly, rowing and sculling were technically advanced sports a long time ago. There have been no fundamental advances in technique for a very long time, nothing, for example, to alter sculling radically in the way that high jumping has been altered. Visible differences between a good sculler today, and a good sculler of twenty years ago—or fifty years ago for that matter—are remarkably small, and mainly due to differences in equipment. The disappearance of the long swing, for instance, was brought about by the introduction of longer slides, not by any planned development in technique.

Secondly, technique is difficult to impart. Professional sculling coaches used to do it by example. But, without intending offence, there are few modern coaches capable of teaching sculling by example. So they try to give a man 'length' by increasing the length of his slide, help a slow or clumsy man to make an effective 'catch' by giving him bigger blades, and so on. I am not suggesting that this is necessarily a bad thing, but simply that it is one of the reasons why 'training', and 'mechanics', now seem to play a bigger part than technique.

Thirdly, the improvements in performances which have

been achieved in the last two decades, have nearly all stemmed, or so it seems to me, from Germany and Eastern Europe, as a result of 'selection by strength and fitness', and of the mechanical developments which have been introduced to cater for very large and very strong (but not always very skilful) men.

I do not quarrel with this trend. It would be futile to do so. But I do believe that, because of the emphasis given to 'physical training', there is too little emphasis given to 'technical training'. It may work in countries where sport is part of the philosophy of life, and platoons of professional coaches can draw on regiments of dedicated young athletes. But I suggest that the ordinary mortals who use this book are not very often going to beat the strong men at their own game, but might sometimes surprise them by turning out to be better scullers.

But that is a digression, to explain why 'technique', rather than 'physical potential', still heads my list of requirements.

Technical Potential. Beginners may improve simply by doing more sculling. But even they will improve quicker, if they learn the right way from the start. More experienced scullers, on the other hand, who have already acquired a personal technique, rarely improve by 'going on doing the same thing for longer'. This is why so many of them flog over our regatta courses, year after year, without ever getting any better.

The more experienced a sculler becomes, the more he needs humility (to recognise the fact that he is not sculling well enough), and thoughtful planning (to work out ways of giving himself a better chance). It is not sufficient to 'try to do it better'. Every aspect of sculling technique, which was discussed in Chapter II of this book, needs attention every year.

As the complete stroke cycle is the sum of all its parts, and as each part interacts on every other part, it is not possible to 'perfect' one part in advance of the others. I suppose that a golfer might set about perfecting his putting, without affecting his driving. But the sculler cannot perfect his finish without attention to his beginning.

This means that technical training must also be cyclic. Many scullers must have noticed the phenomenon that, when they start sculling in the autumn, after a couple of months rest, everything will go gratifyingly well. But after a few days their sculling seems to get worse instead of better. What is really happening is that some part of their stroke is getting better, and adversely affecting another part. 'Adversely' is perhaps not the right term. It cannot be 'bad' to improve the catch. But if improving the catch makes the boat move faster, and this results in the sculler getting his hands caught up at the finish, he may well think that something has gone wrong, rather than right.

So, in the autumn, the sculler should give himself a complete refresher course, working through every aspect of technique, the way he holds his sculls, his 'three-point suspension', approach to the catch, co-ordination of swing and slide, draw at the finish. He should cover everything, but at the same time, having carried out a careful analysis of the previous season's sculling, and decided where any damaging weaknesses lay, he should pay special attention to these points. Since he cannot watch himself in action, photographs, cine film, and other people's observations, are invaluable in this task.

This process should be written into the training programme, so that concentration is focused on some specific point, say for a whole week. It will be written into the daily programme, too, for specific attention during certain pieces of work. But, because of the interaction of different parts of the stroke, the sculler must move on to another point, after a few days. This process of 'working round the stroke cycle' should generally continue throughout the winter and spring.

Physical Potential. It is not necessary for me to state that a sculler's performance is limited by his physical, as well as by his technical potential. Indeed, if I have a mission, it is to persuade him that the technical side is important too.

When I wrote *The Oxford Pocket Book of Sculling Training*, I devoted a considerable part to training, including circuit training, weight training, and so on. This was a major purpose of that book, written a decade ago, when there was very little literature aimed at the use of these routines for sculling and rowing. The scene is different today. I have most of the A.R.A. Training Pamphlets, for example, and I note that there is one devoted to rigging, one entitled *Learning to Row* (3½ pages of text!), one entitled *Coaching Methods*, and no less than eleven dealing with 'Training in and out of the boat'.

This seems to me to speak for itself, particularly if one reflects on the not very noticeable success achieved in recent years. But it clearly indicates that it is not necessary for me to devote much space to 'physical training'. It is all there, in pamphlets which every A.R.A. member should have. So I confine myself to basic principles, and comment.

Strength. Every time you use any set of muscles you cannot avoid acquiring 'strength'. Certainly you build up strength while you scull in your boat.

But sculling, in itself, does not call for great strength (it is only sculling fast and winning races against tough opposition which demands strength). So, by just sculling along the river, you do not acquire a great deal of new strength. Furthermore, if you try to do it 'too hard' you are likely to do it rather badly. Maximum effort is not conducive to good technique.

So it is really much better to try to acquire strength out of the boat, rather than in it. Fortunately it is also easier and quicker. For on dry land you can select activities which put the maximum work load on the muscles which you want to develop, and you can give them more work, in ten minutes, than you could give them in an hour in the boat, without putting your sculling technique in jeopardy.

Strength is a long term project, and must therefore be an objective during the winter and spring. At the risk of using unprofessional language, I would say that strength is acquired by increasing the load, rather than the duration of the work. By running upstairs in a pair of hob-nailed boots you will make it seem easy work when you next run up with bare feet.

Any intelligent person can apply this knowledge to strength training, according to the facilities at his disposal. Or he can study the many books and pamphlets available on the subject. I have only two comments to add. I would like my pupils to remember that they are aiming to become strong scullers, and not candidates for a Mr. Universe Contest. Huge biceps will not win sculling races. Also I am of the opinion that it is dangerous to use weights *for strength exercises* (which entail heavy loads) without expert training, and constant expert supervision.

Stamina. Stamina, although an aspect of strength, is quite different from strength as such. Many people have great stamina, without much strength. Both strength and stamina, of course, are functions of mind as well as of muscle. But this is particularly true of stamina, which I might describe as both 'the will and the ability' to go on.

As we have very little 'sprinting' in rowing and sculling (perhaps unfortunately from the spectators' point of view), stamina is even more important than strength to the sculler.

To return to that staircase, we can acquire stamina by walking up and down all day, without recourse to running, or wearing hob-nail boots. Or to return to my unprofessional language, we acquire stamina by increasing the duration, rather than the load, of work.

It is easier to acquire stamina, than strength, whilst sculling. Indeed it is impossible not to do so. And we can, and indeed must, plan to do some of our stamina training in the boat. But stamina is a function of mind as well as of muscle. You need to go far beyond the point of tiring your muscles, to the point when the concentration of the mind is breaking down—and then force yourself to go on—and on. And, since good sculling is also a function of the mind, this inevitably means that good sculling will then be at risk. So here again it is convenient to do some part of our stamina training out of the boat.

In the boat, stamina training takes the form of intervals, repetitions, and long distance work. The advantage of intervals and repetitions is that the 'rest periods' give the brain an opportunity to regain control. If you were to try to scull, at the sort of intensity which you use on a 2,000 metres course, for, say, 6,000 metres, you would probably not succeed. But if you did succeed you would certainly be sculling very badly before you reached the end. And remember that, just as every good stroke you scull makes it likely that you will scull the next stroke well, and tomorrow's strokes well, so every bad stroke makes it likely that your sculling will deteriorate. So you just cannot afford to scull 'to exhaustion' too often, during practice. But if you substitute a series of 500 metres repetitions, with short recovery periods in between, you have a good chance of retaining your form as well as your work intensity.

This is perhaps the moment for a word of warning about repetitions and intervals, and indeed about ultra-long sculling at high pressure. There is nothing new about any of these practices, and they all have their uses. But I sometimes wonder if sufficient thought is given to the implications of the huge cumulative work loads which are now commonly used. And I am not only thinking of the formal repetitions, but also of the habitual—one might almost say compulsive—repetitive work which goes on. For example, on a day which is scheduled for a 'light outing', one frequently sees crews (and no doubt scullers do the same), proceed for several miles, alternating say 1 minute maximum pressure with $1\frac{1}{2}$ minutes of paddling, and so clocking up 10–15 minutes of allegedly 'maximum pressure' work, without even registering the fact. One knows quite well what they are after. But one sometimes wonders whether they have thought it through to its logical—or illogical—conclusion.

The human body has a built-in defence mechanism. Long before it reaches exhaustion it 'closes down' the systems which supply energy to the muscles. Furthermore it has a finite supply of energy available at any given moment. 'Training' is simply 'conditioning' the body to do what we ask it to do.

It is perfectly true that 'stamina training' has the effect of progressively increasing the body's work potential. *But if we regularly condition the body to expend all its resources over a distance of, say, 6,000 metres, can we expect it, at the flick of a switch, suddenly to expend all its resources over 2,000 metres?*

I ask the question, rather than offer the answer. But my conclusion is that stamina training, in the boat, should not be pushed too far, and that the 'rate-of-work-demand' should not greatly exceed the 'race-work-rate-demand', at least in the last few weeks before racing commences.

As a salutary demonstration of the meaning of phrases such as 'work rate', 'maximum effort', 'full pressure', and so on, I recommend the following training exercise. First try sculling one single stroke *as hard as you can possibly do it*. The body's in-built inhibition against doing something as hard at it possibly can, will probably mean that you have to try several times, before you achieve a stroke of a violence which you can accept as being 'maximum effort'. Then try to see how many such strokes you can scull in succession. You have to be very determined about this, and scrupulous in not cheating yourself, because you are asking your body to do something which it never normally does, and which, in point of fact, you have probably conditioned it to regard as 'bad' (since the strokes you scull will almost certainly be rough, bad, strokes). So your body will tell you that it is doing it quite hard enough, when you know this not to be so. When I first evolved this exercise I found that eight or nine strokes was the longest sequence I could manage, without being conscious that the effort was falling off, and therefore less than 'maximum'. The most I ever achieved, much later and at the height of training, was about twenty strokes—and that was very exhausting indeed, leaving one panting and palpitating.

I think this is a useful exercise, as a reminder that we are using 'double talk' all the time, particularly when we use terms like 'maximum', and 'flat out'. It is also worth remembering this exercise when we are congratulating ourselves on having put in an even bigger mileage than usual, or a longer period of 'rowing' than usual. The late Steve Fairbairn said 'Mileages makes champions', and that phrase passed into our language. And of course he was absolutely right, in an era when 'work loads' were pretty small. But is it really the mileage, or the number of minutes, which makes the champions? Or is it perhaps the *intensity* of the work? Anyway, this is another awkward question which it is worth thinking about on a rainy day.

To return to stamina training, there is an enormous choice of out-of-the-boat stamina exercises and activities, in the A.R.A. pamphlets and elsewhere. There is no need for me to prescribe specific exercises. But take care that all groups of muscles are covered.

There is not the same objection to the unsupervised individual using weights for stamina training, as there is in strength training, because he is now concerned with cumulative, rather than immediate loading. The only reason for increasing the load is because it becomes tedious, and time consuming, to do too many repetitions of the same exercise. The safe rule is not to use more weight than can be handled without difficulty.

Spread the Work. I believe that it is better to spread the work throughout the day, when this is possible, rather than to rely on one concentrated training session. Some loosening-up exercises, and a short run before breakfast, make a useful start to the day. Walking to and from work, and in the lunchtime break, is also indicated. Isometric exercises are possible at all sorts of odd moments during the day. Strictly I am incorrectly using the term 'isometric', which means exercising the muscles without moving the load. If, sitting at your desk, you take hold of each end of the desk, and try to 'squash' it, that is 'isometric'—unless you succeed, of course, in which case it may be just plain expensive. If you sit with your knees apart, with hands on the knees, and try to close your knees together with your leg muscles, whilst pulling them apart with your hands, that is isometric too. There are innumerable such exercises which you can devise, to exercise different muscle groups. And there are many other exercises, which are not isometric, which you can practise wherever you happen to be. For example, you can go through the sculling movement with your arms, exaggerating the roll back of the shoulders and the drop of the wrists. Or you can slip in a dozen quick knees-bends, or chin-ups, on the architrave of the doorway.

Running and Walking. The preoccupation with sophisticated equipment, and modern training methods, often leads us to forget the simple things in life. It is actually good for you to walk to the station, rather than to take a bus, particularly if you walk briskly, with controlled breathing. And the staircase is much more profitable than the lift. And running is probably the finest all-round exercise of all. I have already said that you should run every morning, before breakfast, quite gently, with a couple of short sprints when you have warmed up. And, at the very least, you should run four or five miles, preferably over undulating ground, on any day when you cannot go out sculling. Run at varying speeds, gradually increasing the tempo as you go, and always exercising the lungs.

Controlled Breathing. In these days it may sound a little trite to say that oxygen is our life support system, or rather the raw material thereof. Our lungs extract the oxygen from the air we breathe, and pass it into our blood stream, which distributes it to our muscles. When we take violent exercise we make increased demands on our lungs. If the demand exceeds their capacity to supply, it first becomes exceedingly uncomfortable, and then we grind to a halt.

We have a saying, 'as natural as breathing', which is worth a thought. For breathing is so natural that most of us never think about it at all, except when we get 'out of breath'. Furthermore, although it is such a vital function, most of us, for most of the time, only do it to the extent that our bodies subconsciously demand it. In fact we only use a fraction of our lung capacity, continuously 'topping up' the top of the tank, so to speak, and letting the main supply get stagnant. Whether this matters medically, in the normal way, I do not know. But in the training context it means that we are not exercising our lungs fully, and our lungs, like all other parts of the body, are quite capable of being trained to operate more efficiently—if they are exercised fully.

It was the holding of the Olympic Games at Mexico City, at an altitude above 7,000 ft., which focused attention on 'oxygen starvation', and the solution was altitude training. And, of course, it was clearly demonstrated that, by working at high altitude, where there is less oxygen, the lungs can be conditioned to process more air, and extract more oxygen. If this discovery was only relevant to competition at high altitudes, it might not affect us too much, since there are not likely to be many rowing and sculling competitions at high altitude. But, unfortunately, it was also demonstrated that the effect of altitude training remains beneficial, for a period, at lower altitudes. It takes some time for the lungs to get 'lazy' again. I say 'unfortunately' because we could well have done without such an expensive discovery. Rowing and sculling cost too much anyway, without having to traipse off for three weeks to some mountain resort, in order to have an equal chance with those who are lucky enough to have mountains on their back door step.

However, I believe we can go a long way towards combating oxygen starvation, without ever setting eyes on the mountains.

Next time you go walking, try to see how many paces you can make one breath last. Do it systematically, breathing in for 5 paces, and out for 5 paces. If you cannot do that comfortably, and keep it up indefinitely, you are in pretty bad shape. So try ten paces breathing in, and ten paces breathing out. If you find that easy, after half a dozen breath cycles, walk a little quicker, or break into a run. Exhaling is what you must concentrate on, pumping the last cubic inch of stale air out of your lungs. You do not need to worry about inhaling, because, when you empty your lungs, and continue to take exercise, your whole body will start screaming for oxygen. The only problem you have then, is to prevent yourself taking a frantic gulp, which will not fill your lungs, and will leave you, before the end of your ten paces, or whatever cycle you are attempting, with no more oxygen to come.

If you will take the trouble to learn 'controlled breathing' it will revolutionise your sculling. As a young man I never had a particularly good 'wind', and I always dreaded the second minute of a race at Henley. We always used to say that there was a vacuum between the quarter-mile signal box and the barrier. It left one gasping and struggling for air, and I have no doubt that it had a disastrous effect on efficiency. Seven years later, when I made a 'comeback' to rowing and sculling, I discovered controlled breathing (I am sure many other people 'discovered' it too, but I cannot recall any coach ever telling me about it). Without any doubt it made all the difference to my enjoyment, and probably to my performance too.

It is not sufficient to practice controlled breathing only when you are doing a land training session. You should try to do it all the time, when you are walking, going up and down stairs, or just sitting at your desk. And practise holding your breath, too. In fact, try holding your breath right now. It is remarkable how few people, even when they believe themselves to be quite fit, can hold their breath for much more than a minute and a half. At this moment, as a decrepit, chronic smoker, I can just manage a minute. When I was preparing for the 1948 Olympics I could do 3—3½ min., and repeat the exercise two or three times, with a dozen deep breaths in between. This was not brave, or clever, but simply because I had big lungs, and *had taught myself to empty them completely, and to fill them to capacity with fresh air.*

Controlled breathing also pays dividends in the boat. I have more to say about this in Chapter VII. But it is no good waiting until you get to 'The Race'. Your very next outing on the river is the time to start breathing in rhythm with your sculling. Breathe in as you take the catch, and out as you slide forward. It is easy for a few strokes, but needs a lot of practice if you are to sustain this pattern for long periods. If you cannot manage it, you will have to take two breaths to each stroke. Some people find the opposite pattern easier, exhaling on the catch, and inhaling as they slide forward. I do not know whether this really matters. But I do know that, one way or another, systematic breathing, in and out of the boat, can greatly increase a sculler's efficiency, and comfort.

General Health. The time is not so very far removed when quite well informed people believed that rowing and sculling were excessively arduous, and potentially dangerous sports. Of course this was nonsense, for rowing and sculling, calling for no violent efforts, and no physical contact between competitors, must be among the least dangerous sports.

Nevertheless it remains true of our sport, as of all others, that they should never be undertaken when 'off colour'. Nor should suspected strains and sprains be ignored.

Diet. When I was an undergraduate oarsman, one of the first things which happened, when we 'went into training', was the appearance of a strict list of what we could, or could not eat. It was probably necessary, as the tendency was to eat too much, and too richly, anyway. When I returned to competition, after the war, eating habits had changed, and rationing meant that the problem was to obtain sufficient suitable food, rather than to avoid eating too much. Without doubt we were much fitter. Precise diet sheets were not much in evidence, and the general rule was to eat regularly, what you were accustomed to eat, and in moderation. Nevertheless, when Dr. Raymond Owen, who is now Honorary Medical Adviser to the British Olympic Association, wrote his admirable book on *Training for Rowing* in 1952, he still thought it necessary to lay down specific rules about feeding.

I do not think that I have the necessary expert authority to lay down dietary rules. But I am often surprised by what I see men eat in training today. It seems to me, for example, that the intake of fat and carbohydrates is often excessive. This may be partly because training sessions in the boat are more demanding than they used to be, and I suspect that the current infatuation with weight, for its own sake, has something to do with it.

One cannot dispute the axiom that 'a good big-un should beat a good little-un'. But, personally, I cannot interpret this as meaning that the same man is better value if he is as heavy as possible, rather than as light as possible. I myself was a big man, at 6 ft. 6 in., and I weighed around 14 st. 4 lb. as an undergraduate. But ten years later I was undoubtedly stronger, and fitter, and weighed several pounds less.

In general, the sculler who is training himself should exercise discipline in his eating habits, and should aim to carry no more than a few pounds of excess weight, a week before Henley Regatta, or whenever his major effort is going to be. By 'excess' weight I mean weight which a couple of days of hard racing will take off, and which will not return unless he either decreases the work-load, or increases his food intake.

Drinking habits in training have also changed, and, I think, not necessarily for the better. All forms of alcohol are now usually forbidden. But the total quantity of non-alcoholic liquid which may be consumed, seems to be virtually unlimited.

I am not going to suggest that alcohol, as such, is good for training. But it seems to me that the alcoholic content of a pint of 1975 beer, for example, cannot possibly have an adverse effect. On the other hand, I believe that the consumption of large quantities of liquid, be it the purest water, is harmful. And as I reckon that most people drink less beer than water, to quench the same thirst, I would rather see a man consume one pint of beer, at training table, than two pints of orange squash.

For what it is worth, my advice is that liquid intake, in training, in normal weather, should be limited to 3—3½ pints a day (say one cup or glass at breakfast, tea, and bedtime, ½ pint at lunch, and 1 pint at dinner). In hot weather the quantities can be somewhat increased. What the liquid shall be is a matter of preference, but avoiding fizzy drinks, and iced drinks. Above all, the practice of coming in from the river, and consuming large quantities of liquid before going in to eat, seems to me to be pernicious.

As regards stronger alcoholic drinks, these, I believe, move into the realms of psychology rather than diet. Personally I believe that an occasional glass of port, as a reward and relaxant, after particularly hard work, is more likely to be beneficial than harmful. The same applies to a couple of glasses of red wine, or champagne, at the end of a hard week. Certainly these are artificial stimulants. But, if they are going to have a good psychological effect, I do not believe that they can be harmful on balance. Black coffee, on the other hand, which is regularly permitted today, seems to me to be less likely to make a man happy, and more likely to keep him awake.

I know that this is not a fashionable view today. But it worked for the last four British oarsmen and scullers who won Olympic gold medals, and I shall be more impressed by the modern 'austerity' regime when it produces comparable success.

Recording Progress. We have now considered how to increase technical and physical potential, throughout the year. It is also important that the sculler should know whether he is making progress, and how much.

So far as technique is concerned, it is difficult for a lone sculler to know how he is progressing. I do not believe that continuous coaching is necessary in sculling. But occasional observation and advice from the bank is invaluable, providing it comes from an expert, and preferably the same expert.

Apart from this, the sculler must necessarily rely on his performance to judge his progress. *This entails keeping a log of his work, and the results achieved.*

The problem is to get results which are valid, because of the constantly changing conditions of wind and water. This is rarely absolutely attainable, since the effect of wind conditions cannot be precisely calculated, though the effect of water movement may be.

The best that the individual sculler can do is to keep a record of wind conditions, and, over a period of time, this should give him a reasonable basis for comparison. At least there should be a fair number of days when he can record 'wind negligible'.

As regards the movement of the water, if our man practises on tidal water it is virtually impossible for him to make valid comparisons, since the tidal flow may be changing all the time. But on rivers above the tide level, the speed of the stream does not, as a rule, alter hour by hour (though it may do so locally, if there is a lot of traffic using a lock).

With these provisos, therefore, the sculler must try to calculate comparable performances by doing set-piece rows with and against the stream. He can then calculate an average *water speed*, in one of two ways:

1. Calculate the *land speed* in each direction, by dividing the distance covered by the time taken. Then, where LSA = land speed against the stream, LSW = land speed with the stream, and WS = mean speed through the water for the two rows, the formula is:

$$WS = \frac{LSA + LSW}{2}$$

2. Or, working with *times* in place of land speeds, where td = time for row downstream, tu = time for row upstream, and T = mean time for the two rows, then the formula is:

$$T = \frac{td \times tu}{td + tu}$$

It is also important to assess, and record, progress in land training, but this should present no problem to anyone who thinks about it.

Preparation for Racing. I have already explained why it is not practical for me to suggest detailed training schedules for different scullers in different circumstances. This is still true when the racing season comes along. It depends on how much time a man has, and what he is doing for the rest of the day. But there is one principle which I have expounded in previous books, which is worth repeating here.

Climax and Anti-climax. I hope we have established that the human body is a creature of habit, susceptible to being conditioned to producing certain reactions in certain circumstances.

Training throughout the winter and spring increases the body's strength, stamina, and skill, and conditions it to accepting a heavy workload. As the time for racing approaches, the work-load may remain quite heavy, but the body must be conditioned to expend all its available energy during the period of time which it will take to cover the racing course. It is no comfort to know that we can easily scull twenty miles, or do 10 × 500 metres repetitions, without losing form, if we are then left behind at the start of the race. In other words, we now need to expend all our available energy in, say, 8 minutes rather than in 25 minutes.

At the same time, the body has also been conditioned to

'recover' after exercise, and then to store up energy for the next demand which is made upon it.

This fact we can now exploit in order to produce a 'maximum effort', at the moment when we really need it. We can do this by what I describe as *Climax and Anti-Climax*. This entails progressing towards a peak work-load, and then cutting back the demand, so that the body will store up energy, which we can release at will.

For example, in the run-up week before a race, we can progressively build up the work-load on Monday, Tuesday, and Wednesday, and cut back on Thursday and Friday, in order to race on Saturday. Similarly, over a longer period, in the four weeks before a major event, each week would follow the same pattern, building up to Wednesday or Thursday, and slacking off before a major effort on Saturday, but, additionally, the second week would be heavier than the first week, the third heavier than the second, and in the fourth week, of course, the work would be reduced.

One can even say that this process extends over the whole training period, with the work-load gradually building up from the autumn to the spring, when the emphasis shifts from strength, and stamina training, to speed training, and then falling off in severity during the racing season, though the racing itself restores the balance.

This method of Climax and Anti-Climax provides a purposeful framework for the training programme. And it should be planned in advance, and adhered to. For, as a sculler becomes fitter and stronger, he feels (and indeed is) capable of more and more work, and is tempted to undertake more and more work. But if he succumbs to this temptation he defeats the object of the exercise, which is to accustom himself to an increasing work-load, and then deliberately to cut down, so as to come to the start of the race full of energy, and keyed up to be off.

Work Load. I have mentioned the pitfalls of terminology in referring to 'work load'. The true work load is not to be measured in miles, or repetitions, or circuits, but in the actual amount of energy expended during the day. In theory this can be scientifically measured, but to do so is not a practicable proposition for the individual sculler.

What really matters, I would suggest, is not the work load which is written into a training programme, but the *recovery* rate which occurs in actual practice. During periods of stamina training, and strength building, it is right, and indeed necessary, that the sculler should be tired, and sometimes exhausted, at the end of a training session. But superficial recovery should follow quickly. Certainly the sculler should feel like going home to a good meal, within 15–20 minutes. At bed time sleep should be welcome, and quick, and there should be complete recovery overnight, so that the sculler, awakening next morning, is eager for another day's work. If this does not occur, and if there is no other obvious explanation—for example any physical indisposition—then the training work load should be reduced immediately.

It must be recognised that failure to recover an appetite for exercise may not necessarily indicate that the training programme, in itself, is too severe. It may be due to other factors, such as employment, travelling, and domestic chores. This is a fact of life, which must be faced. If there are too many other unavoidable commitments, then success in sculling will not come easily. If the sculler is only to be satisfied with success, in terms of winning races, it is better to face the fact, at the outset, that this sort of success is only to be had, if time, and energy for the necessary training, are available.

VII

THE RACE

IT IS IRONIC that the estimable Baron de Coubertin, founder of the most fiercely competitive of all sporting events, should have declared that the important thing is not to win, but to take part. However that may be, most of those who take up sculling, do race, and do wish to win. In the nature of things, most of them cannot win very often. But if they are going to devote so much time and effort to their training, it is a pity if they do not at least do themselves justice when they go out to race. If the fastest man always won, sculling would be less exciting than it is. But that is no reason for not wishing to see every man give of his best. Here, then, are a few suggestions for those who wish to succeed.

Form. Always study your opponent's form, and, if possible, conceal your own. An unexpectedly fast start, an unforeseen ability to spurt, an unprecedently strong finish, can often be decisive.

The Course. It helps to know the course, particularly the average, tortuous English course. Even on the straight, international type courses, conditions are rarely identical on all stations, at all points on the course. Be aware of the prevailing wind and water conditions throughout the race. This may sound obvious, but many a sculler has lost a vital length by 'slogging on into the headwind', when in fact he has run into a patch of sheltered water. To be aware of the changing conditions, and to profit from them, is the mark of the sculler whose brain remains in control.

The Start. It is important to know exactly how much time is needed to reach the stakeboats. A long wait can be just as upsetting as a frantic rush to get there in time. Always allow time for warming up, which should include several bursts at racing pace.

About a minute before the start, take a series of a dozen deep breaths, concentrating on complete exhalation, to clear the lungs of stagnant air. No advantage is gained by taking more than a dozen such breaths. Above all, do not forget to breathe when the race starts. This advice may sound ridiculous to some. But, in the excitement of the moment, many men do just this, and wake up to a state of acute oxygen starvation at the end of the first minute. Therefore condition yourself, in practice, to breathe deeply, in rhythm with your sculling, inhaling at the beginning of the stroke and exhaling as you slide forward. If you cannot maintain this pattern you must change gear, and take two breaths to each stroke. Somehow or other you must get that air, and go on getting it. Resistance to exhaustion is directly linked to oxygen intake, which can be dramatically increased by practice.

Race Tactics. The sculler must know his own capabilities, and it will help if he also knows his opponents' capabilities.

It is generally reckoned that the quickest way to cover a given distance is to scull at an even pace, which will mean husbanding strength in the early stages, and consciously and progressively increasing the pressure over the second half of the course. But an 'even pace', even if it really is the 'best pace', will not guarantee success. Indeed, on courses which have large bends, it may be quite the wrong tactics, particularly if the lanes are not buoyed. The geography of the course is all important.

Even on straight, buoyed courses, there is scope for tactics.

As on the running track, the man who prefers to set the pace must be sure that he is fully extending the opposition, unless he is absolutely confident that no one else can match his finishing power. Even more so, the man who favours a 'waiting race' must be sure that he is not losing contact, and that he can catch his opponent before the finish.

It follows that in multi-lane racing the sculler has to be sure which of the other contestants poses the real threat. One may habitually rush off, and grind to a halt after a thousand metres. Another may hold back, and the whole field believe that he is out of the race, only to be shattered by a devastating finishing spurt. On multi-lane courses many scullers lose through racing against the wrong man.

And what of the men who really are evenly matched? For them, 'contact' is the over-riding consideration, for neither can afford to let the other get away. Even if they know that the pace cannot be maintained, they must go on together, until one or the other breaks.

And this brings me to my last word on tactics.

Grandstand finishes please the spectators, but earn no prizes—unless they are successful. A man comes to the start of a race with just so much strength and energy to expend. Perhaps, psychologically, he can squeeze out a little more than he *realised* he possessed. But he cannot squeeze out more than he actually possessed. If he races himself to a standstill, and is beaten, that is that. And it ought to be a matter for congratulation, not for condolence. For no man can do more. But if he saves himself for a grandstand finish, and crosses the finishing line full of fight, closing the gap, but still in second place, that is the most unsatisfactory conclusion to a race he can possibly achieve. For he has proved to everyone else, if not to himself, that he has lost a race which he might possibly have won. If some of those cheers are for him, then they are the ignorant cheers.

How much better to have 'had a go', while there was still time, and to sleep easily that night, in the knowledge that he was beaten by a faster sculler, rather than by himself.

VIII

WOMEN'S SCULLING

WHEN I WROTE THE SYNOPSIS of what this book was to contain, the chapter heading 'Women's Sculling' slipped from my pen in all innocence. I planned no confidence trick, to obtain a few more sales. But when I had written the first seven chapters, and came to this one, the truth dawned on me.

'If, within the limits of the space available, I have said all I want to say about men's sculling', I asked my conscience, 'what is there left to say about *women's* sculling?' For that matter, should I perhaps have written another chapter, headed 'Sculling for Schools', and netted a few more unwary customers? The fact is that there is not really anything new, or different, to say.

Superficially, one might perhaps think that because women are usually less strong than men, it should be possible to develop a thesis that they have need of a special, and more highly developed technique, to compensate for lack of physical strength. But everyone, irrespective of sex and strength, needs the best technique that he or she can acquire, in order to reach the top. So one could as well argue that, if it is strength that a woman lacks, she should devote more time and effort to physical training, and less to technique.

Personally, I do not believe that this is so. Women compete against women, not against men. Therefore all, metaphorically, are 'in the same boat'. A stronger woman has the advantage over a less strong woman. But equally, a more skilful woman has the advantage over a less skilful one. So we are really back at square one. To succeed, you must strive to become 'the complete sculler', male or female.

Of all the subjects covered in this book, the one which seems most likely to require divergences is that on rigging. Strictly, I do not think there are necessary divergencies, since, as I have already pointed out, rigging is simply the art of fitting the boat and equipment to the requirements of the sculler, and this remains true, whatever the sculler's size or sex. Nevertheless, it is true that the Rigging Table, on page 16, is specifically drawn up for scullers between the heights of 5 ft. 6 in. (167 cm.) and 6 ft. 3 in. (190 cm.). To adapt it beyond that range it is only necessary to adjust the figures *pro rata*, using a little common sense. But it may perhaps be helpful to look at it here, from the point of view of women scullers, say between the heights of 4 ft. 6 in. (137 cm.) and 5 ft. 6 in. (167 cm.).

Heels above bottom of boat. This is only a marginal measurement, in any case. But it would reduce as the size of the boat reduces, say to about $1\frac{1}{4}$ in. (3 cm.).

Seat above heels. This, too, would reduce *pro rata*, as the boat itself, and the sculler using it, becomes smaller. For a sculler of 4 ft. 6 in. (137 cm.), a reduction of about 1 in. ($2\frac{1}{2}$ cm.) might be expected.

Work above seat. This is primarily a 'comfort factor', aimed at providing a convenient clearance of the hands over the thighs, during the recovery. With a smaller boat, and a smaller sculler, one would expect a smaller measurement. But the reduction will not necessarily be *pro rata* to the men's requirements. For example, a sturdily built adult woman might require relatively more clearance, over the thighs, than a boy, or a young man of similar height.

And this may be a suitable moment to digress to a special problem which many women scullers must face, at least in countries where women's sculling does not enjoy the same financial backing which is forthcoming for men—the fact that they may have to make do with boats which were built for heavier and larger scullers. If a boat is carrying a load which is less than that for which it was designed, it will float high in the water. And, since the sculls' blades must still be buried, at the same point in the water, this means that the scull handles will be higher above the seat of the boat.

This problem may occur whenever scullers use boats which were not built to their own particular specifications, and this is why my Rigging Table allows for variation in the height of the work. In the case of a girl using a boat built for a man, a measurement well outside the range which I have suggested, might be necessary. The only advice I can give is that, if the work has to be set at anything below 2 in. (5 cm.), it is certain that the boat is much too large for the person using it.

Frontstop and sliding distance. A shorter sculler must surely have shorter legs, and will therefore necessarily slide a shorter distance (p. 22). So, for scullers in the 4 ft. 6 in.–5 ft. 6 in. (137–167 cm.) range, the 'sliding' distance is likely to be between 15–17 in. (38–43 cm.). The position of the frontstop—I use the term not to describe the actual physical stop, of course, but the point to which the sculler slides forward—is still dictated by the setting of the stretcher, and need not necessarily be different for scullers of different heights. But if one assumes that the 4 ft. 6 in. (137 cm.) sculler is also going to be less strong than the 5 ft. 6 in. (167 cm.) sculler, and will therefore be moving her (or his) boat, less fast, then there will be less difficulty in catching the water at the beginning of the stroke, and therefore less need to slide forward 'through' the work. About 1 in. (2½ cm.) might be more appropriate than the 1½ in. (4 cm.) suggested in the Rigging Table.

Span. The span should continue to reduce, as in the Rigging Table, by approximately 1 in. (2½ cm.) for each 3 in. (8 cm.) of height.

Sculls, overall and inboard. The sculls must continue to fit the span in accordance with the I : S formula (p. 32). It may be argued that the smaller sculler, having smaller hands and being more compact all round, can do with less overlap of the scull handles. But since overlap, in effect, means leverage, I doubt this. The OL measurement should remain at or near 8–9 in. (20–23 cm.).

The Inboard : Outboard (I : O) ratio (p. 33) however, can well be reduced to provide more leverage. For scullers between 4 ft. 6 in. and 5 ft. 0 in. (137–153 cm.) an I : O ratio between 1 : 2.35 and 1 : 2.40 should be correct.

Blades. I have already suggested that many male scullers use blades which are unrealistically large. It follows that if women make do with blades built for men, they are likely to be severely overloaded. A blade of the currently standard length of 19–20 in. (48–51 cm.), having a width of 5–5½ in. (13 cm.) at the tip, and a maximum width of 6–6½ in. (17 cm.) at a distance of 6 in. (15 cm.) from the tip, gives a profile area of approximately 100 sq. in. (645 sq. cm.), which should be a suitable general purpose woman's blade.

Work load for Women. I have written elsewhere about the pitfalls surrounding the phrase 'work load'. By my definition—that work load is not to be measured in miles, or repetitions, but in the actual amount of energy expended—

a woman must obviously have a lighter work load than a man. But it does not follow that she must scull over the course less often, do less intervals or repetitions in practice, or attempt fewer sets of exercises in land training. For her work load is automatically scaled down by the fact that she is preparing for a shorter race, using less severe rig, and, in land training, using exercises and equipment appropriate to her own strength.

I have sometimes produced training programmes, and advice, for individual women scullers. But, again at the risk of being repetitive, I cannot offer specimen programmes here, because what might be suitable for one reader, preparing for the Women's National Championships, might be quite unsuitable for another, lower down the scale, and *vice versa*.

But the principles suggested in Chapter VI remain valid, not least that the key factor in considering work loads should be the recovery rate. It takes hard work to become a successful sculler, and the harder the work the greater the success is likely to be—providing there is full recovery between training sessions, and continuing enthusiasm to get back to work.

Sculling is an ideal sport for women. There has been a good deal of nonsense talked about 'femininity', and the objections to women participating in competitive sport in general, and rowing and sculling in particular. It seems to me that it is visibly evident that femininity has very little to do with taking part in sport. The Russian gymnast, Olga Korbut, became a symbol of femininity overnight. Yet, at the time of writing, her free programme has been ruled to be too dangerous, and there is a possibility that she will give up competitive gymnastics. No doubt this will break some hearts, but I doubt that it will increase her feminine appeal.

I suppose that no active sport can be completely devoid of

any risk of injury. But sculling, being a non-contact sport, with no bats, balls, racquets, or other lethal implements involved, and calling for no sudden violent effort, must be among the safest. Even the muscular strains which one encounters in sculling, can, more often than not, be traced to activities out of the boat, or perhaps to lifting the boat in an unguarded moment. Sculling cannot even be accused of producing unsightly or unbalanced muscular development.

It has always seemed to me that one of the most unfair arguments is that women ought not to indulge in activities which they cannot pursue gracefully and well. Goodness knows, if the same argument were applied to men, our regatta entry lists would look a bit thin.

Of course there are scullers of both sexes who are ungainly and unsuccessful. But there have also been some extremely good women performers on the river, especially in sculling. In the 1972 National Championships, for instance, I reckoned C. M. Davies and M. H. Gladden, as possibly the most accomplished scullers in the entire championships. If our British women have not often excelled internationally, it is surely because their facilities, and financial support, have fallen far short of those enjoyed by the men, particularly when compared with the support given to women's rowing and sculling in some Continental countries.